This is a journey of discovery into a largely uncharted landscape. Through repeated set-backs, misunderstandings, conflicts and struggles, one campus Christian community is faithful to a commitment to overcome division and history with integrity. The lessons these students and their leaders learn along the way go far beyond issues of race to confront issues of community, justice, identity and the boundary-defying nature of the Good News of Jesus Christ.

Reverend Ian Oliver, Senior Associate Chaplain for Protestant Life, Yale University

Honest truth was spoken and real love practiced. Nobody got what they expected and ev-erybody received more than they ever dreamed possible.

Reverend David Midwood, Pastor, Bedford Community Church, Bedford, New Hampshire

...the authors...share about both the blessings and the hardships that come from seeking after Christian unity amidst diversity. If you believe that the church is called to demon-strate that racial reconciliation is a critical part of its witness to the world—or perhaps if you need to be convinced of this fact!—then this book is for you.

Helen Lee, Author, The Missional Mom

The book is a home-run, bringing together a great blend of voices highlighting faith in Christ and how that works itself out in real ways in community... I would very enthusi-astically recommend it to pastors and church leaders—both those who were embarking on multiethnic journeys, but also those who weren't necessarily thinking in that direction.

Reverend Jennifer Oraker Holz, Associate Pastor, First Presbyterian Church, Colorado Springs

Readers will be challenged to develop communities on earth that will mirror what will be true in heaven as individuals from every tribe and nation gather to worship the one true God. Developing communities of trust in which different cultural needs and experiences are valued and the whole Gospel lived out for others requires sacrifice, commitment and dependence upon God. The journeys of those who have travelled with the Amherst Chris-tian Fellowship not only provide a picture of possibilities but challenge each of us to take the next step in our own circles of influence.

Dr. Randy MacFarland, Provost and Dean, Denver Seminary

Confronting racism is more than a notion. It is very complex and elusive...[A Trans-forming Vision] provides enough Biblical evidence that would cause any opponents to take a second look.

Jimmy McGee, President at The Bitumen Group Inc., Atlanta

It makes me question whether we are doing enough to be multiethnic or whether our church/elders are even aware of the issues as presented in this book...I thoroughly enjoyed reading it, and learning from it!

Jan Davis, International Coordinator, Mustard Seed Missions

An extremely important book that moves racial reconciliation beyond a collegiate intellec-tual exercise and provides a real world example of Christian community that successfully crosses racial boundaries.

Reverend Stacy Riely Pardue, Meredith College Chaplain, Raleigh, North Carolina

A Transforming Vision tells a compelling story of one campus fellowship's journey to take the call of the gospel to heart and practice living and loving as Jesus taught in the middle of the secular campus. The lessons they learned changed not only the students who tell their stories here but the practices of those who followed them. Thank God for the risks they took under Paul's leadership to live out the glorious, challenging, metamorphic invitation to follow Jesus.

Chris Nichols, Regional Director, InterVarsity Christian Fellowship, New England

Wow! Rarely have I found a book to be simultaneously full of rebuke, instruction, inspiration and encouragement... As the National Director of The Navigators Collegiate Ministries from 2003 – 2008 I have seen both the value of and the need for exactly what this book is about – the intentional pursuit of multiethnic expressions of faith, friendships and fellowship both in campus ministries and in local churches.

Mike Jordahl, City Life National Director & 20s Leader, The Navigators

There have been few who have attempted to capture both story and systemic issues, principles & tactics in multiethnicity all in one book. It's clever, in that it draws in those who learn by story as well as those who are looking for practical principles and next steps.

Marcia Wang, Associate Director of Multiethnic Ministries, InterVarsity Christian Fellowship/USA

It is a must-have handbook for anyone who has a heart for breaking down the invisible walls that separate the body of Christ. It reveals important information for both the layperson as well as clergy.

Darlene Gibson, speaker and writer, North Kingstown, Rhode Island

For those groups, whether campus or church based, struggling with the issue of multiethnicity (or lack thereof), here is an unsanitized but authentic and inspiring account of why it has to be a priority and how to go about making it a reality.

Sven Soderlund, Professor Emeritus of Biblical Studies, Regent College, Vancouver, British Columbia

As a student involved in the Amherst Christian Fellowship, I was inspired by Paul's unrelenting passion for racial reconciliation. Now, serving with a multicultural college ministry, I can see even more clearly the challenge of bridging the divide. Reading these poignant stories of students and faculty convicted me to transcend my own prejudice with love.

Jennifer Pei, Leadership Development Associate, Epic Movement

What a great look into the Kingdom of God! I loved each of the early chapters in the first half of the book, as diverse people shared their stories of how God changed their lives and built them together in a Christ-centered, multiethnic fellowship... The second half of the book reminds us that we still have a long ways to go. Our church needs to "go to school" from the insights and wisdom of how to honor and care for one another, while pursuing the kind of unity that demonstrates to the world whose we are.

Reverend Doug Whallon, Pastor of Discipleship, Grace Chapel, Lexington, Massachusetts

A Transforming Vision

Multiethnic fellowship in college and in the Church

Edited by
Paul V. Sorrentino

Doorlight Publications
South Hadley, Massachusetts

Doorlight Publications
PO Box 718, South Hadley, MA 01075
www.doorlightpubs.com
info@doorlightpubs.com

First published 2011 by Doorlight Publications.

Cover art by Lauralee Harrington

Author Photo: Steven Vote

Cover photo used by permission of Getty IMAGES

ISBN 978-0-9778372-7-4

Printed in the United States of America

To members of the Amherst Christian Fellowship
Past, present and future

We loved you so much that we were delighted
to share with you not only the gospel of God
but our lives as well, because you had become
so dear to us (I Thessalonians 2:8)

ACKNOWLEDGEMENTS

It has been an enormous gift for me to work with the contributing authors of *A Transforming Vision*. I had the privilege of spending time with them when they were at Amherst College, as either students or staff. Years later, we were able to pour ourselves into this project which means so much to all of us. I thank God for our continuing partnership and friendship.

Many people have helped us along the way. Jean-Luc Charles kick-started this journey when he agreed to begin meeting with me and Dan Glaser in the summer of 1993. We have been friends ever since. Priscilla Kelso, Tibby Dennis, Alexis Spencer-Byers, Jessica Hahn and Eric Olson-Getty all provided significant input. The Reverend Dr. Alice Brown-Collins has been very influential in my thinking through her teaching, friendship and prayers. Mrs. Hermenia T. Gardner has been a mentor to me in all of the areas discussed in this book as well as a dear friend and prayer partner. Spencer Perkins and Chris Rice have been teachers for all of us directly or indirectly. Their friendship, writing, and example have been foundational to my thinking. It was at the Reconcilers' conference that they hosted in Jackson, in 1998, that I felt called to make racial reconciliation a lifelong calling. That commitment was reinforced after Spencer's death a few days later.

I am grateful to my InterVarsity supervisors who helped me process this material and supported my slightly atypical approaches to ministry at Amherst College over the years: Doug Whallon, John Ratichek, Rich Lamb, Scott Brill and Chris Nichols. Members of my "Culture and Ministry" class at Bethel Seminary of the East were enthusiastic, able and thoughtful conversation partners as I taught this material for the first time.

I have been encouraged and supported by my friends in the Thursday morning CC-Riders book group from College Church. Dawn Murry has been a friend, assistant and reader of every manuscript variation. My dear colleagues in the Offices of Religious Life and the Dean of Students have been both supportive of my writing and patient with me as I took time away to work on this project. Luca Grillo, Frank Couvares and Ilan Stavins have each provided encouragement.

I could never say enough about Dan Brown and Doorlight Publications. Dan believed in this book from the start and he has provided perspicuous insight and recommendations on the manuscript. He has also worked tirelessly and incredibly hard to see this book go to print. I am very grateful.

My father, Dr. Louis V. Sorrentino, read through the entire manuscript and offered incisive comments. More than that, he surprised me by taking some of the material to heart and demolishing the maxim that "you can't teach an old dog new tricks." I thank God for my Dad.

I owe my deepest debt of gratitude to my wife Karen. She has put up with my many quirks for thirty-four years and somehow managed to maintain a sense of humor and be a constant and loving support. I am proud of my two boys, John and Tim; they have been a great source of delight for me and I am thankful for their presence in my life.

Paul V. Sorrentino

South Deerfield, Massachusetts

November 23, 2010

CONTENTS

FOREWORD
CHRIS RICE
"THE AMHERST MOMENT"

In a rich essay about the Letter to the Ephesians and its powerful image of Christ overcoming "the dividing wall of hostility" between Gentiles and Israel (Eph 2:14), theologian and missiologist Andrew Walls describes the letter as emerging from an unprecedented historical moment. In a real place called Ephesus, in a small, fledgling church community, Greek and Jew dared to share social life together over a period of time which altered them forever—their ways of seeing the world, their core identities, their vision of following Christ.[1]

Writes Walls of the letter's message:

"Only in Christ does completion, fullness, dwell. And Christ's completion, as we have seen, comes from all humanity, *from the translation of the life of Jesus into the lifeways of all the world's cultures and subcultures through history. None of us can reach Christ's completeness on our own. We need each other's vision to correct, enlarge, and focus our own; only together are we complete in Christ"* (italics mine)

The discovery at Ephesus puts a startling claim on the lives of all Christians: "The very height of Christ's full stature" (Eph. 4:13), writes Walls, "is reached only by the coming together of the different cultural entities into the body of Christ. Only 'together,' not on our own, can we reach his full stature."

This "Ephesian Moment," as Walls calls it, is now the crossroads of Christian history in the 21st century. And what is at stake is nothing less than growing into the full stature of Christ.

Across America, across the world, the cultural and economic ground is shifting beneath our feet. A friend in rural Iowa tells me that their school district, all-white for decades, is now majority Latino, and has thrown

---

1 Andrew Walls, "The Ephesian Moment" in *The Cross-Cultural Process in Christian History* (Maryknoll, NY: Orbis Books, 2002).

them into confusion. We are in a global time of unprecedented migration and immigration, of increasing traffic of missions groups and initiatives from the U.S. to Africa, of European nations struggling with who will be in and who will be out, of a U.S. crisis over a broken immigration system.

Yet as Ephesians testifies, it is exactly at such times and places and borders, throughout history, that the Holy Spirit brings interruptions of new possibilities and communities of new creation, in unexpected places, among ordinary people, who become a sign of hope in their world.

What we greatly need to find are stories of "Ephesian moments" breaking into our own turbulent time, stories about borders of separation becoming seen and embraced as gifts rather than divides which remain hidden or resisted. Such stories correct and enlarge us, and within them we will find the resources for being shaped into God's "new we"—wisdom, faithful practices, spiritual disciplines, ways of engaging and resisting the "powers" both seen and unseen which keep us captive.

A Transforming Vision comes to us for exactly such a time as this.

From the unlikely ground of highly-selective Amherst College in western Massachusetts, a place where we don't expect the "best and the brightest" to choose any path other than upward mobility, a very different story happened over the years shared there by a group of students, faculty, and staff.

Like those at Ephesus—from diverse cultural backgrounds and socioeconomic histories—they arrived at Amherst with imaginations of self-sufficiency. But as one of the key instigators, Paul Sorrentino, puts it in this book, "God had much bigger plans for us. We never knew how good it could be: how rich the relationships and how much broader our vision for what it means to be a follower of Jesus would become."

"We never knew how good it could be." That is exactly the point, especially given how difficult it was, and is, to dare to come together across lines of difference. Central to the power of the story told in *A Transforming Vision* is to illuminate the kind of concrete, down-to-earth changes which are nec-

essary if this new life is to take hold of us. They learned that how power is used, who makes decisions and how, can be either a means of grace which releases the Spirit and the gifts of all, or blocks transformation by holding power in the hands of dominant and often implicit structures. They learned to see that we have all been habituated to remain apart, to think we can live well and find the truth about the world (or Christ) self-sufficiently, to assume we do not need each other. What they learned is that even how we sing and pray is not innocent but is culturally formed, and that learning to offer these gifts to one another is hard work. But like different musical "sections" which are rich in themselves but only find their full meaning and completeness in symphonic chorus, if we can learn life together the music is far more beautiful.

The story-tellers use the language "multiethnic." I dare say there is more going on here: strangers (and, in some ways, enemies) growing into a profound and surprising interdependence, becoming a new reality, even a new mestizo of in-between people whose hyphenated and supposedly "fixed" cultural identities (Asian-American, African-American, Haiti-American, white-American, etc) were further hyphenated and confused through their shared social life toward a transcendent end: Christ-likeness. These are changing people and identities which beg for a new language.

I had the great joy of sharing in this story. I'll never forget the pleasure of standing knee-keep in snow with my colleague Spencer Perkins the first time we arrived in Amherst from Mississippi. And I'll never forget that, unknown to them at Amherst who drew so much from our words and presence, our two journeys to Amherst were during two of the most fragile and difficult moments in Spencer's and my own relationship. But we always tried to be authentic. When we did, when we do, somehow the Holy Spirit shows up in spite of ourselves. As a friend once put it to me, "racial reconciliation is the best ground I know of to die to self and to know Christ." We must *be* the change we seek in the world.

Let us not underestimate the powerful ripple effects of "Ephesian moments" and "Mississippi moments" and Amherst moments," of ordinary people in small, fledging places being made new by sharing life together. Walls contends that the Ephesian moment, "the social coming together of people of two cultures to experience Christ," was brief. But when intense enough, when enough risk is undertaken, when enough intimacy and trust is established, brief can change us forever.

From this deeply-shared historical moment, people were changed forever and left Amherst, scattered by the Spirit across the world to plant themselves in ministries of justice in Washington DC, in inner city community in Mississippi, in teaching in a public school in Boston, and in going into places of power yet with a taste and vision for building the beloved community.

As Paul says in this book, this story is not about a new church program but "an entirely different way of doing church." And, I would add, a deep way of being formed into Christ for such a time as this in our changing U.S. and global landscape.

This book is the story of the "Amherst Moment" — the translation of the life of Jesus into the many cultures which converged at Amherst and began to make of them a new people, a new culture. In it we glimpse what is at stake, why it matters, and what it might take to get there in our own communities, institutions, and congregations.

And why it is worth it to plunge into the journey. Only together are we complete in Christ. This makes everything worth it — the awkwardness, the discomfort, the sacrifice. In fact, it makes the journey itself beautiful, a journey into holiness, a journey into releasing the fruits of the Spirit into our lives—love, joy, peace, patience, kindness, goodness, self- control (Galatians 5:22). For such a time as this.

INTRODUCTION

REVEREND PAUL SORRENTINO

In the summer of 1993, I sat with several InterVarsity Christian Fellowship staff members watching a training video on multiethnic ministry. InterVarsity, as a national movement, was beginning to emphasize the need for us to examine the place of ethnic minorities in our fellowships and to consider how they were being incorporated into our fellowships. The video featured an InterVarsity staff worker named Barbara. Barbara was an African American woman whom I had met at a national conference. She was highly respected throughout InterVarsity, and she was especially known for prayerfulness, gentleness, hospitality and godly wisdom. I was shocked by what I saw on the screen.

The video tape we watched that day had been recorded in 1992, shortly after the Rodney King court verdict.[1] The recording showed Barbara speaking at the podium. She was not quiet, meek, or calm. She was outraged, angry, and loud. She found the verdict and, what's more, the reaction—or more accurately the non-reaction— of the white, evangelical church, incomprehensible.

I remember Barbara screaming that "every black church in America talked about the Rodney King verdict" the following Sunday. I was stunned. When was the last time I remembered anything in the news being talked about on Sunday? I surely did not hear anything about Rodney King in my local church that Sunday or any other Sunday. In fact, I would have been

---

1 In March 1991, George Holliday captured home-video footage of Rodney King, an African American, being severely beaten by members of the Los Angeles police force. Up to a dozen officers were present. On April 29, 1992, riots erupted in Los Angeles after a jury decision was announced, on live television, that the four police officers accused of the beating had been found innocent.

surprised and maybe annoyed if something had been said, and I would have thought it out of place. Wasn't that more of a political issue that should not be talked about in church? Aren't there lots of opinions and perspectives on this issue? Who was I to judge? I liked the sanitized version of church. I did not want anything too controversial to distract me from worship of God through music, prayer, witness and, perhaps, service.

Nevertheless, there was Barbara. Screaming! I had met her. She worked for the same ministry I did and cared about the life and faith of students just as I did. Or was it just as I did? Why was her reaction to the Rodney King beating so different from mine? I was upset at first, too. Then I heard the explanations. I followed the news reports. Rodney King was a big man. He had been on drugs. The drugs made him stronger than ten men. There was a rational explanation for why these officers, the "good guys," did what initially seemed so inhumane. Barbara was still screaming. She felt strongly about this, more strongly than I could understand. Why was this godly woman in such a different place than me? Why were our views so different?

In 1963, after a speech at Western Michigan University in Kalamazoo, the Reverend Dr. Martin Luther King, Jr. was asked, "Don't you feel that integration can only be started and realized in the Christian church, not in schools or by other means? This would be a means of seeing just who are true Christians." Dr. King replied:

> As a preacher, I would certainly have to agree with this. I must admit that I have gone through those moments when I was greatly disappointed with the church and what it has done in this period of social change. We must face the fact that in America, the church is still the most segregated major institution in America. At 11:00 on Sunday morning when we stand and sing and Christ has no east or west, we stand at the most segregated hour in this nation. This is tragic. Nobody of honesty can overlook this. Now, I'm sure that if the church had taken a stronger stand all along, we wouldn't have many of the problems that we have. The first way that the church can repent, the first way that it can move out into the arena of social reform is to remove the yoke of segregation from its own body. (King 1963)

Should Dr. King's concern in 1963 matter to us four decades later? After all, a black president has been elected. Do we still need to be concerned about race? When immigration issues are polarizing the country, do Christians have a path to offer that gives dignity to our neighbors and bridges the divide? When whites in the United States will no longer be the majority by mid-century, do we consider what influence that should have on our local churches? Should the church have something to say about ethnic conflict, cleansing and genocide around the world? Should Christians be involved in providing a solution and setting an example that unites instead of divides people?

I believe that the Christian church must play a leading role in overcoming divisions of race, ethnicity, culture, and class that keep us separated and that serve to elevate one group at the expense of others. I believe this is the way of Christ. This book is about how the church can follow that way. It is the story of what happened to a small Christian fellowship in the years 1993-2005, and it is a story about what it means to be a faithful follower of Christ in fellowship with people of other races and ethnicities. It is a window into lives that were transformed and lessons that were learned at Amherst College, a small, private liberal arts college in western Massachusetts. The vision of a multiethnic fellowship that we gained in our life together has endured as students have graduated and moved into churches. For us, it has been a transforming vision and we believe it should be for the church today.

A Transforming Vision is not a political book. It is not about red states and blue states. At heart, it is a book about what it means to fulfill Jesus' prayer for his disciples in John 17:23: "May they be brought to complete unity to let the world know that you sent me and have loved them even as you have loved me." The unity of God's people, across denominational, racial, ethnic, class and other lines of difference, is God's intent and serves as a testimony to the reality of Christ's incarnation and God's love. Conversely, a divided church provides a weakened and anemic witness to the watching world.

This is not a book about political correctness. In fact, it would be best to forget about the confines of political correctness for the sake of reading this book and discussing it. Talking about racial matters is always challenging. We worry about how we will say things and if we will offend someone. The reality is that we will make mistakes, and we will offend. We must recognize that as part of the learning process and be patient with one another, for as the Apostle Peter wrote, "Love covers over a multitude of sins" (I Peter 4:8).

A Transforming Vision is about why Christian communities should be multiracial and it provides a practical vision of how that can take place. The contributing authors all had a common experience in an intentional multiethnic fellowship through their involvement with Amherst Christian Fellowship at Amherst College over a thirteen year period.

The Amherst Christian Fellowship, affiliated with InterVarsity Christian Fellowship since 1981, has been an intentional multiethnic fellowship since early 1994. The membership during that time period has fluctuated between 31 and 90 students.[2] I served as the primary InterVarsity staff worker during those years.

All of the contributors, except for me, have now left Amherst College and continue to follow Christ in local churches. Several serve as pastors. One has returned to Amherst to serve part-time as a religious advisor. Although the story is told through the eyes of particular people at a particular place and time, we are convinced that the principles learned there have a crucial role to play in other church and parachurch settings. The contributing authors' experience in their ministries today bears this out,

---

2 See Appendix 1 for a detailed breakdown of Amherst Christian Fellowship composition over the thirteen-year period.

and research on multiracial congregations, reviewed in chapter 8, is consistent with our own experience.

Each writer is convinced of the benefits of a multiethnic fellowship for the sake of the people involved and for the effectiveness of our outreach. Collectively, we affirm the thesis of the authors of *United by Faith*: "when possible, congregations should strive to be multiracial" (DeYoung, Emerson et al. 2003, 12).

A Transforming Vision is divided into two major sections. The first section offers personal narratives. Each writer shares a different perspective on how he or she was affected by involvement in a multiethnic fellowship, and each has a dramatic story to tell, reflecting his or her background as an African American, Chinese American, Cuban American, mixed heritage as European & Chinese American, and European American.

The second section addresses the kinds of changes we found necessary to make in our fellowship if we were to function well as a multiethnic body. We begin with research data on the reality of the racial divide in the United States. Then we discuss more practical aspects of a multiethnic fellowship, including structures, relationships, leadership and music. The section ends with a concluding summary and closing reflections.

The chapters can be read independently. There is a logical sequence, but it is not essential to read the chapters in order. Our intent is that the stories in the first section should be complimented and explained by the theory and practice in the second section.

The book concludes with five appendices containing a variety of resources. Appendix 1 is an overview of biblical passages related to multiethnic fellowships. Appendix 2 provides data on the make-up of the Amherst Christian Fellowship during the years 1993-2005. Appendix 3 discusses the reasons it is sometimes valuable for a congregation to be ethnic specific and not multiethnic. Appendix 4 is a Bible study in the Book of Acts that focuses on crossing cultural barriers. It is divided into ten studies. Appendix 5 is a listening exercise that provides the opportunity for two people to get to know some significant things about one another.

Finally, I should say a word about terminology. "Multiracial," "multiethnic" and "multicultural" are often used interchangeably. We have tended to use "multiethnic" in this book, but not exclusively. We chose to use multiethnic as a way to acknowledge that the broader racial categories have important subcategories. There is a difference, for example, between black people whose family roots are in Africa, the Caribbean or the United States. Examples of ethnic groups are Vietnamese, Mexican American, Chinese and Irish. Multiracial is a handy reference because it clearly indicates that we are looking at broad categories of difference such as black, white, Hispanic and not simply Swedish or Danish. Multicultural is an even broader category than multiracial and multiethnic and generally includes any type of diversity (e.g. this may include such categories as rank and class, gender, sexuality and orientation, ethnicity, race, physical abilities, age, language and national origin). Our focus in this book is narrower so we have primarily used multiethnic and multiracial.

A Transforming Vision builds on established research on multiracial congregations and illustrates these principles through stories of people involved in a successful multiethnic fellowship over a period of years. It should be of special interest to those who would like to see their own congregation, youth group or campus group become more multiethnic. It is our hope that reading this book will convince you of the breadth and depth of the racial divide and of the benefits of being a bridge-builder across that divide for the sake of Christ. May God help us to fulfill Jesus' prayer in John 17:21 "that all of them may be one."

PART I
OUR STORY

We humbly request your company on a journey.

Embarking on a journey is always an adventure. Even if we plan every detail, we never know what unexpected turn of events will change a dull trip into a life-changing experience. That was the case for all of the contributing authors of this book. Most of us began the walk into racial reconciliation and multiethnic fellowship with a sense of obligation. It was one more thing that we needed to do on our check-off list as followers of Jesus. It would soon be over, and we could get back to life as usual.

God had much bigger plans for us. We never knew how good it could be; how rich the relationships, and how much broader our vision for what it means to be a follower of Jesus would become. We are so very grateful to God for inviting us to come along. That is what we now ask of you. Come along with us on this continuing journey. You may begin with mixed emotions and reluctance. You may be unsure if you really want to take this trip. Isn't that the way with most good things? Just when you are about to begin, you have second thoughts. The comfort of your own home seems more attractive and inviting than stepping off into who-knows-what. But we invite you to come along as we share our story.

It is *our* story. Stories provide a window into who we are and what we are about. In this section, nine people tell what happened in each of their lives as they entered this journey. It was not what any of us expected, but it was and is good. God changed us through what we experienced together. These first seven chapters, woven together, represent one story of what God did in a small Christian fellowship and what the Lord continues to do in each of our lives.

Of course, the ultimate adventure is being a follower of Jesus. No part of that journey is boring or unimportant. But there are aspects of the trip that are exceptional. That was the case for us. What we thought would be a brief, side excursion turned out to be a vital part of how we are to live as Christians. We never knew. We invite you to come along with us for a journey that, for us, has become a transforming vision.

1

How we began

Paul Sorrentino

In the summer of 1993, entering my final year of seminary, I attended a chapel service that did what chapel services are supposed to do. It changed the trajectory of my life and started me on a journey that continues today. The speaker was Ted Ward, professor of educational ministries and missions at Trinity Evangelical Divinity School. I was not prepared for what he said.

Dr. Ward talked about the Reverend Dr. Martin Luther King, Jr., and his call to the church in the '60s. Dr. Ward said that the white, evangelical church had been minimally involved in the civil rights movement. He provocatively asked if the church would respond any differently today. He asked us if we would be willing to become reconcilers and peacemakers. Ward said that racism was the single most important issue facing America. He provided plenty of documentation. I had no idea. I considered racism a significant issue, probably in the top twenty, but hardly number one. Like many white evangelicals, I seldom thought about race matters. That began to change on that summer day in 1993.

That chapel service with Ted Ward together with Barbara's passionate response to the Rodney King verdict moved me to action. My own thinking was far removed from the positions being taken by these two Christian leaders, but I was convinced that I at least needed to do some study in this area to become better informed. InterVarsity Press had just published a book by Spencer Perkins and Chris Rice entitled, *More Than Equals*: *Racial*

Healing for the Sake of the Gospel. All InterVarsity staff members were encouraged to read it.

I wanted to read and discuss the book with a person of color. Jean-Luc was the president of the Black Student Union at Amherst College and had some involvement with the Christian Fellowship. Although I did not know him well, I really did not know any other black students and thought he might be my only option.

When I met with Jean-Luc at the campus center I could not have imagined what I was really asking of him, or what I would be getting into myself. He graciously agreed to meet with me every other week to discuss *More Than Equals.* We were joined by a third person, Dan, a white student leader in the Christian Fellowship. In retrospect, it was good that there were three of us, since it placed less pressure on each of us and meant that no one was "on the spot."

Our format was simple. We each read the chapter for the week, and then we each responded to the chapter. Our weekly meetings became increasingly important to each of us. We were not only discussing our week's chapter. We were learning to share our lives together. We were in the process of becoming friends or, as Perkins and Rice liked to say, yokefellows.

One of the major lessons I was learning was that majority people can focus on race issues any time we want and for as little or as much time as we want. Racism is such a non-issue for us that it is easy to spend little or no time thinking about it. That is not true for our brothers and sisters of color. Meeting with Jean-Luc and Dan meant that I had to consider the issue of race at least once a week. I had to do the reading, and that made me think about racial reconciliation. What made me do much more, however, was my growing friendship with Jean-Luc. I find that it is hard to think about prejudice and racism in the abstract. I can so easily fool myself into thinking that I do not have a racist bone in my body — that I am much better than I am. It is much harder to do that when my friend endures the effects of racism every day, and he is sitting in front of me.

Perkins and Rice had organized their book into three major sections: Admit, Submit and Commit. The Admit portion of *More Than Equals*, called for an awareness of a problem. I was coming to recognize and acknowledge a deep-seated prejudice within me that seemed bottomless. I was learning that I needed, and still need, to spend time with people of color if I am to get beyond my own rationalizations about how good (read non-racist) I am and face up to the lies I have come to believe about those different from myself. This was not an easy admission.

This lesson was brought home forcefully to me in an incredible story told by Spencer Perkins in *More Than Equals*. Spencer had gone to a Christian college on the west coast. During his first semester, he had become very close to a white, first-year student. They were seen together regularly. The College even used their photograph in promotional literature. They spoke about rooming together. Then his white friend's roommate left college. Spencer naturally assumed that they would become roommates. Perkins remembers his friend's words when he returned to campus:

> "I've decided that it will be best for us not to room together." Aware of my bewilderment, he continued, "It has nothing to do with you. I like you and would love having you here, but I don't think I could handle your black friends hanging out in here."

Perkins recalls his devastation:

> What was he saying? What was wrong with my black friends? Did being accepted by whites mean that I would have to give up my black friends—my blackness? Had I assimilated so much that now Dick could think of me as white? But I wasn't white and like many blacks in that era, I had grown to be proud of my blackness (Perkins and Rice 1993, 86).

This story has remained vivid in my mind ever since I first read it. It was made more horrific by Perkins' interpretation of the experience. Black friends had warned him repeatedly about getting too close to white folks. A high school friend had provided Spencer with this summary assessment: "There is a little snake in all white folks" (Perkins and Rice 1993, 85).

From the time I read Perkins' nightmare account, I pledged that, to the best of my ability, and by God's help, I would never violate a trust like that with anyone. One of my professors used to say, "God is good at bringing good things out of their opposites." I wanted to be a part of God's redeeming of Perkins' hurt. While I may not be able to fully rid myself of the snake, I can commit to doing all in my power to minimize its effect on others. By God's grace, I can be a dependable, trustworthy person who follows through on what I say I will do. Having someone's trust is one of the greatest gifts anyone can give. I want to be a good steward of that gift when I am fortunate enough to receive it. This has become a principal goal in my life.

Not long after our discussion of Perkins' white friend story, the Inter-Varsity campus groups in western Massachusetts held a retreat at a camp about 30 miles from the College in a remote area, at a relatively high altitude. Jean-Luc had responsibilities that kept him on campus after the rest of us had left to caravan to the camp. I was delighted to see Jean-Luc walk into our meeting room later that night just before I was to speak. After the meeting ended, Jean-Luc pulled Dan and me aside. We stepped outside where it was cold, but where we would not be overheard. Jean-Luc asked forgiveness of Dan and me. He said he had not been honest with us. He had recently realized that he had been living in two worlds. One world was when he interacted with whites. This was mostly surface interaction, and everything was usually okay. The other level was when he was with his black friends. With them, his conversations went much deeper. In our regular talks together, everything had been all right because he was operating on the first level. In the past couple of days, God had been convicting him and showing him his deep-seated anger toward whites. He was not sure of just what to do with that, but he knew this was the first step. Jean-Luc took the initiative to be vulnerable and honest, as he would on many other occasions. He had plenty of excuses to return to campus that night, but he slept over at the camp. We discovered later that he had stayed in spite of having no blanket, pillow, toiletries, or other clothes. It was a powerful statement of his commitment to Dan and me, and to the Christian Fellowship.

In the weeks to come, we heard more clarifying stories. Jean-Luc told us how terrified he had been to drive up to the camp for the retreat. It was not simply fear of being lost. He was driving a typical college student car that was near the end of its lifespan. He was frightened by the strong possibility that his car would break down. Once that happened, in that pre-cell phone era, he would have to get help from someone. He was afraid that he would need to approach the door of a nearby house. He was a black man, in the dark, in a white neighborhood. I had never in my life had a similar thought. I had not needed to fear what he feared.

Jean-Luc told us how he was reluctant to walk down the street in the Town of Amherst at night. He just never knew how he would be treated and was apprehensive that a group of angry white kids might attack him. He told stories of going into stores to shop and routinely being harassed, followed by security and frisked. In the past, I would have thought that these stories were exaggerations. The speaker was either making these things up or vastly overstating what happened. But this was Jean-Luc telling me. I had come to know and love him. He was intelligent, conscientious, honest, and unimaginably friendly. Who would do that to him? Yet, this was his reality, and a reality that he was generously allowing Dan and me to enter.

Within the context of our relationships, we were each, especially Dan and I, learning about what seemed like another dimension of our universe, a dimension richer than we could imagine and one that had largely been invisible to us. Jean-Luc was our teacher and guide.

It was inevitable that we should begin to think about the implications of what we were learning for the structure and functioning of Amherst Christian Fellowship. We had intentionally restrained ourselves from considering the broader picture until we had had at least a semester to wrestle with the issues ourselves. Now, the three of us were motivated to work with Amherst Christian Fellowship toward becoming a more diverse, welcoming group.

Jean-Luc and Dan began to co-lead the Fellowship's worship team. We decided to make racial reconciliation the focus of one of our Friday Night Fellowships, our large group meeting, early in the semester. We publicized it well and had an attendance of 30 or so students, slightly larger than our normal Friday Night Fellowship in those days. We met in a lounge that had a relaxed atmosphere. Several new people were there, and interest in the subject was strong. Jean-Luc, Dan and I led the meeting. Jean-Luc and Dan co-led the worship. Jean-Luc talked about the meaning of racism in the church and told his story. Dan addressed Jesus prayer for unity in John 17 and the problem of white solipsism. White solipsism refers to the uncanny ability of the majority culture to focus only on ourselves, a luxury that is not much of an option for ethnic minorities. I talked about what our relationships and studying together had been teaching me. I also spoke about the oppression of blacks as the "big elephant" in the room that Christians need to address. We emphasized that "tolerance," a popular word on campus, was an inadequate response to the Gospel. The Greatest Commandment meant going beyond mere tolerance or even equality to an emotionally engaged, volitional choice to love God and to love our neighbor.

After the meeting, Jean-Luc and another student asked me, "What next?" We did not have long to wait. Almost immediately, three Asian Americans,

Margaret, Sue, and Suhna, approached. They asked if they could lead "Racial Reconciliation 2" the next week. The following Friday night 60 percent of the students in attendance were people of color.

A further answer to "what's next?" followed when we began a series of informal meetings. These meetings were usually held on a Saturday night and would take place at our home. We initially called them "fudge ripple," a term we pirated from Raleigh Washington and Glen Kehrein (Washington and Kehrein 1993, 131-133), and later "full spectrum." We would usually meet for a few hours, beginning with a meal. After the meal, we would introduce a topic (how things were going in the Fellowship; the importance of family; interracial dating) and break up into ethnic-specific groups to discuss the topic. One rule we kept was that participants needed to be willing to have whatever they said in ethnic-specific groups repeated in the larger, multiethnic group. After an hour or so, we would come back to the whole group to discuss what had been said in the ethnic-specific groups. These meetings were an invaluable way for us to expand our understanding of one another.

A pivotal time in the life of Amherst Christian Fellowship took place in February of 1995 when Chris Rice and Spencer Perkins, the authors of *More Than Equals*, came to campus. It would be hard to overestimate the significance of that weekend for the future of Amherst Christian Fellowship. While I had been preoccupied with preparations for a series of lectures by John Stott, Alexis Spencer-Byers, a student leader, had taken charge of the Perkins-Rice event. Alexis tells her story in the next chapter.

2

TAKING THE PLUNGE

ALEXIS SPENCER-BYERS

One of the first Christians I met when I arrived at Amherst College in the fall of 1990 was Jean-Luc Charles, a Haitian American guy with a mile-wide smile.

Here is how it happened: I had written out several of my favorite Scripture verses on index cards and posted them around my dorm-room door, raising eyebrows among my non-Christian hall mates. One evening, as I sat at my desk, studying, I heard running footsteps come down the stairs and past the entrance to my room. Then I heard a screech of rubber soles on linoleum, followed by a few slower steps in the opposite direction. A moment of silence, and then Jean-Luc's head poked through the doorway.

"Are you a Christian?" he asked.

"Yes," I answered. We have been friends ever since.

We both became involved with the Amherst Christian Fellowship. As a white-Chinese woman who had just spent four years at a magnet high school in the San Francisco public school district, I found the racial make-up of the Fellowship—mostly Asian American and white, with a few African American and Hispanic members—quite familiar and comfortable. I didn't notice right away that many of the black members only attended sporadically, and I didn't wonder how the Colombian Bible study leader felt about being the only Latino at most of our gatherings.

My first clue that there might be something missing in our corporate theology came during my sophomore year. A group of minority students locked themselves into an administrative building and presented the College with a petition requesting certain changes, including adding an affirmative action officer to the school's payroll, and offering more courses focusing on ethnic studies. I was eating dinner one evening with a few friends from the fellowship when a student approached our table to ask if we wanted to add our names to the petition.

I didn't think long about the request. Raised by liberal, non-Christian, socially conscious parents, I had great respect for the civil rights movement and non-violent protest in general. I signed the petition. My tablemates did not. Afterwards, we sat in silence for a while. Opposing questions jousted in my mind: "What's the matter with them?" and "Uh-oh, am I a bad Christian?"

I don't mean to suggest that the Fellowship or its members were intentionally excluding or ignoring minority students. But we had not yet really begun to wrestle with how our faith should inform our perspective on race and justice issues.

In January 1994 I returned to Amherst after a year off and started hearing Paul, Jean-Luc, and Dan talk about a book they had read called *More Than Equals*. Intrigued, I bought a copy to read over the summer. A few pages in, I was hooked. "Anything like this in SF?" I scribbled in the margin beside a description of Voice of Calvary Fellowship, a non-denominational interracial church in Jackson, Mississippi, engaged in inner-city community development work such as housing rehabilitation, health care, and youth ministry.

Back on campus in the fall, I dove headfirst into local racial reconciliation activities. Amherst Christian Fellowship was planning to bring Perkins and Rice to town to lead a workshop. I agreed to serve on the planning committee. Jean-Luc and a few others were attending a Church of God in Christ congregation in Springfield. I joined the carpool. When a Bible

study started up in Charles Drew House, Amherst College's black culture
house, I began attending it.

As fate, or God, would have it, everyone on the Perkins-Rice committee
who had seniority over me left the team to handle other fellowship-relat-
ed responsibilities. I was left in charge of pulling the workshop together.
Armed with a multi-page to-do list, I set about rounding up a sponsoring
team including the Black Student Union, the Gospel Choir, the Affirmative Action Office, the International Students' Association, the Asian Culture House, and the President's Office. By February, we were ready to
welcome our guests with a multicultural extravaganza that exceeded all
expectations.

At our kick-off event on Friday night, a white man introduced the Gospel Choir; an Asian woman introduced Jean-Luc, who shared his reconciliation testimony; and then I introduced Spencer Perkins and Chris Rice
with words that would prove true for me: "I think you'll find, if you really
sit down and take this book and this message of reconciliation seriously,
that it will impact every area of your lives." Following the talk, we ad-
journed to Drew House for a hybrid meal of ribs and lo mein, prepared by
the Black Student Union and the Asian Culture House, and for a performance by the Christian a cappella group, *Terras Irradient*.

On Saturday, we left music and food behind us and got down to business with an all-day workshop, during which Spencer and Chris expanded
on their three principles of admitting, submitting, and committing. After
church on Sunday, I drove Spencer and Chris to the airport, which gave us
roughly an hour to talk. How these men had the energy to interrogate me
after such a full weekend I will never know, but their series of questions
unearthed these vital pieces of information: I was a senior, I was an English
major, and I did not yet have firm plans for life after graduation. From this
profile, Spencer made quite a leap: "Why don't you come to Jackson and

do a year-long internship with us?" he suggested. He and Chris were planning to write a second book and would need someone to provide editorial assistance on the project. They also put out a quarterly magazine called *Urban Family*. They thought I would fit right in.

Four years of InterVarsity training had prepared me for a moment like this. "Hm. I'll definitely pray about that," I agreed. What I meant, of course, was, "There's no chance in [the hot place] I'm going to move to Mississippi…but I'll let you guys down easy." However, I try to be a woman of my word, so my prayer partner and I began to mention this off-the-wall possibility to God at our twice-weekly prayer sessions. Before long, she and I each independently came to the conclusion that I was, in fact, supposed to go to Jackson.

My parents, who completely understood my desire to do work in the inner city, did not exactly understand the notion that God was "leading" me to venture into the Deep South. Nevertheless, they found it within themselves to be supportive of my decision. I ceased my efforts to be accepted into a teaching program and signed up for a subscription to *Urban Family*. "It's just for a year," I told myself frequently. "It'll be an adventure, and then I'll get back on track."

In the meantime, amidst the "highs" associated with the workshop and all the new people I was meeting, things I was learning, and culture I was experiencing, a few hard realities of cross-cultural involvement were beginning to make themselves felt. I did not last very long at the Church of God in Christ church. My friends who had been going there had stopped attending; for a while I continued by myself, but I never could get comfortable with the worship style—songs that went on and on with nary a lyric in sight, multiple offerings that involved walking up to the front of the sanctuary, jumping, and so on. There was nothing wrong with any of those elements of worship; they were just completely foreign to me, and I was still a beginner in my efforts to appreciate and incorporate the unfamiliar into my own worship life.

Not wanting to give up on the ideal of interracial worship, I asked around and found out that several African American Amherst students were attending an AME Zion church within walking distance of campus. I shortened my Sunday morning commute, resumed worshipping with classmates, and found a church that was ethnically different but liturgically similar enough to my Presbyterian roots that I could concentrate more on God and less on worship style. I was well accepted by the congregation. At least one person there interpreted my beige skin as part-black, and that might explain why people didn't see me as out of place. I finished the year there quite happily.

After graduation my mother and I boarded an Amtrak train bound for Chicago, changing there for the City of New Orleans. We stepped off the train into a dreary gray station on the edge of downtown Jackson. Although we arrived an hour late, our ride was later. We had time to take in the surrounding area, which consisted mainly of empty lots and dilapidated buildings, including a massive and long-abandoned hotel. I would later hear conflicting stories about the 1967 closure of the hotel, a casualty of white Mississippians' resistance to desegregation.

Eventually, Mom and I were picked up and transported to the neighborhood in west Jackson where Voice of Calvary and *Urban Family* were housed. As we explored over the next couple of days, we were surprised by the decidedly non-inner-city feel of the neighborhood. Single-family homes on tree-lined streets were separated by large yards. I dubbed it "suburbs with burglar bars" and was rather disappointed. Over time, I would recognize that, appearances aside, west Jackson exhibited many inner-city characteristics— a high crime rate, slow response time by law enforcement, prevalence of drugs, dearth of (legal) businesses, and low median household income. Early on, though, I felt certain that I had made a wrong turn somewhere around Memphis.

Mom left that Friday. On the following Monday I sat in a room with nine other interns as an African American woman named Lee Harper led us in a Bible study. By the time Lee was done teaching, I had made up my mind that she would be my next "discipler." Being brave enough to inform her of this plan was another matter. It was not until the fall that I actually approached her about mentoring me. She said yes, and we began meeting weekly to study the book of John, to pray, and to get to know each other.

About halfway through my internship year, a group from Amherst Christian Fellowship came to Jackson for ten days of volunteer labor and Christian community development training. I was assigned to shepherd the group through their time with us, and Lee was one of the speakers I invited to address the group. She was slated to do an evening study on the book of Nehemiah, classic community rebuilding material! I was excited for Lee to meet some of my friends from school, and for them to meet her. Then suddenly, the day before she was to speak, I became nervous about her speaking style. I enjoyed listening to her teach. Her study of Scripture was always insightful and helpful, and I loved the animated way in which she imparted the truths she had been learning. Having studied Ebonics (then called Black English) at Amherst, I also had a deep appreciation for the historical and cultural factors that contributed to the deviations from "standard English" that appeared in her speech. But I was worried that my schoolmates would not have the same reaction. I was afraid that they would think she sounded "uneducated," or worse, "unintelligent." On top of that, I was concerned that they would question my choice of a mentor and think less of me. I squirmed through the hours leading up to Lee's talk in a mess of anxiety, guilt, shame, and fear, occasionally even being so petty as to pray things like, "God, please don't let her say 'Deuteromody.'"

My concerns were unfounded. My fellow Amherst students immediately recognized Lee's spiritual maturity and appreciated her vitality and commitment to Jesus, to Mississippi, and to reconciliation and community renewal. It was a great evening. But while my anxiety and fear dissipated, my shame and guilt grew stronger. It was several weeks before I found the courage to confess to Lee what had gone through my head. I will never forget how awful it felt to stand in the doorway of her office at Voice of Calvary Family Health Center, where she was the administrator at the time, preparing to acknowledge my sin against her. I will also never forget how wonderful it felt when she was gracious enough to forgive me, and we were able to continue on our journey as even better friends.

That journey lasted much longer than the one year I originally expected to spend in Jackson, thanks in part to Lee. God used one of Lee's Sunday School lessons from the Book of Ruth to challenge me to make a longer-term commitment to this group of believers who were trying so hard to love God, love one another, and love the community around them through development ministry.

Although it was difficult and painful to decide to spend more time far away from my family, I felt more certain than I usually did about how God was leading me, and I experienced a profound peace as I agreed to follow. When my internship was over, I took a staff position at *Urban Family*. When funding became an issue a few months later, Lee hired me as a receptionist at the health center.

Within a few months, Lee began serving as the interim CEO of Voice of Calvary Ministries, and I had a new job as her executive assistant and coordinator of the ministry's volunteer program. A couple of years after that, I became the ministry's associate director of development when the development director experienced a family tragedy. At every turn, I found myself trying my hand at something I had never done before and being stretched—spiritually, emotionally, and intellectually.

After three years at Voice of Calvary Ministries, I was exhausted. I also saw that, ironically, my employment at a ministry was preventing me from actually "doing ministry" among my neighbors. I quit my job. It might have been logical to move back to California at this point, but I had never felt like my deepest commitment was to Voice of Calvary Ministries. It was to the associated church, Voice of Calvary Fellowship, a ragtag bunch of folks who barely agreed on anything but loved each other anyway, and who were bound and determined to do the work of the Kingdom.

During the twelve years that I was at Voice of Calvary Fellowship, I always felt that the congregation's greatest strength was the diversity of its membership. I cannot begin to measure the extent of the growth I experienced as a result of being in a faith community along with men and women whose backgrounds, experiences, and perspectives were so different from mine. I sat at tables with people who, a few decades earlier, wouldn't have been allowed to sit at a table with someone like me, and I heard their stories of suffering, courage, despair, fear, hope, and progress. Racism became less and less abstract as I saw people I loved and respected receive substandard treatment in business and customer service contexts.

The value of being a member of this multiethnic worshiping community extended beyond the lessons I learned about race. Many of the people who became part of my life because of our mutual involvement at Voice of Calvary Fellowship were simply more spiritually mature than I was. I was profoundly grateful for the opportunity to sit at their feet and to learn from them, not only because of how they could educate me about justice-related matters, but also because they could help me grow in my faith and in my understanding of how God would have me live as a member of His family. If for no other reason (and there are plenty of other compelling reasons), I would be a proponent of racial reconciliation because of my selfish desire to broaden the pool of potential mentors and co-laborers. There is no doubt in my mind that multiethnic fellowships like Voice of Calvary Fellowship, and like the Antioch church described in Acts 11, represent God's desire for His people. There are many passages of Scripture that speak to the centrality of reconciliation—between humans and God, and also among humans— to the Gospel message. The Bible has convinced me that it is right, and experience has taught me that it is good, for Christians of diverse backgrounds to gather together and worship our God. As we do, I believe that He is pleased, our lives are enriched, and the world around us has an opportunity to see the power of the gospel at work.

After the years we spent working together at Voice of Calvary Ministries, Lee and I did two additional significant things together. The first was to open a community coffee house. For several years, we read and saved and planned and prayed and went to Coffee Fests and attended Smoothie Workshops and drove all over our neighborhood, looking for the perfect place to locate our coffee house, which we named Koinonia, the Greek word for fellowship or community. We eventually settled on a dilapidated old home on the same block as Voice of Calvary Fellowship. Then, we spent a year trying to get financing and another couple of years in renovations. Finally, after eight years of preparation, we opened Koinonia.

Four months later, the economy crashed. Starbucks closed most of its Jackson-area locations, and we knew that going under was our likely future. But God gave us favor in the form of a diverse and extremely loyal base of customers who shared our vision for both economic development and racial reconciliation. Blacks, whites, and others came from around the corner, across town, and occasionally from other parts of the country to support this venture. Koinonia recently celebrated its second birthday. This little coffee house has grown into an oasis—a bustling gathering place surrounded by empty, overgrown lots. It is a visible reminder that God does have a knack for bringing streams in places that look suspiciously like wastelands (Isaiah 43).

Though I have since moved back to San Francisco, leaving Koinonia in Lee's hands, I believe that our deep friendship was vital in creating this kind of a place in our community. People could see, just from looking at the two of us and hearing our story, that this would be a space where all kinds of folks would be welcome. Because Lee and I embraced and learned from our differences—she grew up black, poor, and Christian in rural Mississippi in the 1950s and '60s, while I grew up white/Chinese, middle class, and "unchurched" in San Francisco in the 1970s and '80s—we were able to build something that didn't exactly match either of our backgrounds, but sought to embody values of the Kingdom.

A second area of partnership with Lee was caring for Gloria and Kortney. When I first came to Mississippi, each of us interns was assigned to a Voice of Calvary Fellowship family. Gloria Lotts and her then-11-year-old son, Kortney, were my family. I'll never forget the first time the three of us went out to dinner. Gloria instructed me to look around the restaurant. I did. Ours was the only racially mixed table in the dining area. "Whenever we do something as simple as this," she told me, "we're making a statement about racial reconciliation." This was the first of many lessons I would learn from Gloria.

Over the next ten years, Gloria and I shared life in any number of ways. We worked together. We served on church committees together. When their community household disbanded, Gloria, Kortney, and another mother and son lived with me for several months. We shared holiday meals. We became family.

When Gloria was diagnosed with terminal cancer in January 2005, she and Kortney needed a place to stay. I didn't have to think long before inviting them to move back in with me. I wasn't trying to make a statement about racial reconciliation. I was simply taking care of one of my dearest friends. I was making my own little attempt to love my neighbor as myself, and because of the choice Gloria and I had each made to be part of an interracial church, my neighbor happened to be darker-skinned than I was.

For six months, Lee and I put our Koinonia plans on a back burner, and we devoted ourselves to doing everything we could for Gloria and Kortney. We were joined in the effort by a dozen or more others—black and white, male and female—who loved Gloria and took turns transporting her to chemotherapy treatments, keeping her company, preparing meals for our household, and so forth. When Gloria died in the wee hours of June 18, 2005, I called the home hospice nurse, as I'd been instructed to do. Then I called Lee, and she called everyone else. By the time the nurse and the coroner arrived, my home was crowded with people of various races and ages who were busy comforting one another, making calls, brewing coffee, and starting to discuss funeral arrangements.

The Bible says, in John 17:23, that unity among Christians will help the world to recognize the love of God. I thought of this verse of Scripture when I heard that the nurse returned to the hospice, after observing the diverse group of folks who had gathered to say good-bye to Gloria, with this simple report: "It was like church."

3

LOOKING FOR EVIDENCE

CHRIS TSANG

God was pursuing me, but I didn't know it.

In the fall of 1994, I arrived at Amherst College for a one-week community service pre-orientation trip in Hartford, Connecticut, with Outreach, the College's community service organization. For the first time I had been confronted with the reality of poverty in America. I had also never been in such a diverse group of people in my life. When I returned from the trip, I felt more settled, having made some friends through the experience. Still, I was nervous when I finally moved into my two-room triple. As I moved my belongings into the room, I saw that one of my roommates had already moved in. I browsed his music and found that he liked Billy Joel, and he had the "Les Miserables" soundtrack. I felt comforted. From the face book we had been given when we arrived on campus, I learned that the music belonged to Victor Hu, an international student from Taiwan. Victor would soon become my best friend in college and his friendship would help lead me to a decision to become a Christian. The first two weeks of college were a blur. I remember feeling deeply homesick and crying in my room from loneliness. All I focused on that year was academics. I did not participate in any extracurricular activities. The question of who to sit with in the cafeteria caused me tremendous stress. I would come out of the cafeteria with my tray, scan the seating area in front of me, and see if there was anyone I knew. The better plan was to call and arrange to meet someone at the cafeteria. I hated the idea of sitting alone. It took great courage to sit down with a group of people I didn't know. Often, I would go with my roommate Victor to meals and we would sit with people who lived on our hallway, international students that he knew, or people from the Amherst Christian Fellowship. The people from the Christian Fellowship seemed friendly enough and I felt at home with them, unlike the other groups where I often felt like an outsider.

I have fond memories from that freshman year of late night bunk bed talks with Victor that ranged from the girls I had crushes on, to religion, to whether I believed in a God and whether that mattered. When I came to college I wouldn't have described myself as a Christian or an atheist, but perhaps as someone with a fuzzy sense that there might be a God. It didn't really make a difference to my life. I also came to college feeling socially inadequate, even though I had excelled in high school and was able to attend a prestigious liberal arts college. I also remember fondly the times that Victor and I would go out the back door of our dorm, and walk to the gym through the snow to shoot hoops. Sometimes we would be the only two people in the gym. Those were special times of freedom and fun that I am still reminded of whenever I am in a school gymnasium. Victor, much better than I in basketball, taught me how to play the game that no one had really ever taught me growing up. Even though he was much better at the game, he always made it fun to play with him. I noticed during our times of playing basketball that something in him gave him freedom to just have fun without being stuck on winning or losing. I wondered if that had to with his Christian faith.

During the year, Victor invited me to Amherst Christian Fellowship Friday night gatherings. I would politely decline. Towards the end of the year came the dreaded "Room Draw" in which we would find out who we would live with the next year. Rumors circulated that this was a time when feelings were hurt, people were betrayed and friendships broken. Victor and I had applied to join the Asian Culture House (ACH). After the interviews I broke down in tears because I didn't feel like my interview had gone well. I wondered what I would to do if I didn't get in. Victor seemed a lock to get in since he was an international student from Taiwan. I was just starting to get in touch with what it meant for me to be Asian American, something I had thought little about growing up in the predominantly white suburbs of Northern Virginia. I felt that I wasn't "Asian enough" to get in. In the midst of this, Victor told me that if I didn't get in he was prepared to withdraw from the Asian Culture House and to enter the room draw with me. I was touched, amazed and comforted by this display of friendship and loyalty. He was willing to sacrifice his own comfort to make sure I didn't feel like I was on my own. Typically sophomores who entered the room draw did not come close to getting rooms as spacious as those in the Asian Culture House.

The summer between my freshman and sophomore year was one of the most difficult times of my life. I had gone to college in Massachusetts far away enough from my parents partly out of a desire to strike out on my own. That summer I stayed on-campus in summer housing to be the student coordinator of the next Outreach pre-orientation trip. I had benefited so much from Outreach that I wanted to give something back to the next incoming class. In the middle of that time, my mom had become ill and had to be hospitalized. I rushed home to find my mom in a hospital bed. It was one of the scariest moments of my life. The world feels unsafe when a parent becomes ill and you face the fear that you might lose them.

As I returned to school in the fall of 1995, I felt an aching loneliness and emptiness in my heart and soul that I longed to fill. All freshman year I had jumped from crush to crush. I had begun to realize that having a girlfriend, which I imagined would satisfy the deepest longings of my heart, would not bring the satisfaction I wanted. During our late night conversations, Victor pushed me to think through whether the emotional ups and downs were worth it and whether a girlfriend could really meet my emotional needs.

Meanwhile, I had become very interested in issues of race and social justice. My interest was initially sparked by my freshman Outreach orientation trip. That interest grew after I took a course my freshman year called "Reading, Writing and Teaching" in which we discussed the educational system in America. I read Jonathan Kozol's book, *Savage Inequalities*. Reading about the disparity in education between urban and suburban public schools in America shattered my perception of America as land of equal opportunity for all where everyone could achieve "the American Dream." That book and my limited experience assisting in a math classroom in Holyoke, Massachusetts, a small urban center nearby, made me angry and moved me to want to do something with my life to challenge this inequity. I began to consider becoming a teacher. I was also beginning to get to know and becoming friends with people who were not white or Asian. Growing up I had never really had any black or Latino friends. In fact, I didn't have any Asian friends either.

That fall Amherst Christian Fellowship sponsored an event on racial reconciliation featuring Chris Rice, a European American, and Spencer Perkins, an African American, speaking about their interracial friendship and mutual experiences. Although I had not wanted to go to previous Christian Fellowship meetings, this one piqued my interest. I thought to myself, "This goes against all the stereotypes that I have of Christians. They actually want to do something with this race problem in the world. I'm curious." The only contact that I remembered having with Christians in high school was a member of a youth group who was somewhat nice to me. In my head I thought "It's just another clique of white people getting together." Christian faith didn't seem to really impact the way they interacted with me. They weren't mean, but neither did they make any effort to reach out to me in an authentic way. The idea of pursuing reconciliation and justice through relationships, as opposed to social programs, grabbed my attention.

I was mesmerized when I heard Perkins and Rice talk about their stories and their struggles to learn to love one another. I would have expected, given conflict they had gone through, that they would have long ago given up on making things work, but they decided that due to their identity as Christians, that they were going to stick it out and be committed to one another. I was intrigued when Spencer Perkins described the process of forgiveness he decided to go through in sticking it out with Chris Rice even though his dad, John Perkins, had been beaten to a pulp and thrown in jail by white people during the Civil Rights Movement. I wondered what could have moved Spencer to want to forgive these people and still be friends with white people after all that had happened. They also discussed the fact that they and their families along with other people had chosen to live in an intentional interracial living community called Antioch in which they pooled all their money together and used it as a community. They discussed their desire to become a positive influence in their immediate neighborhood through their interracial church, Voice of Calvary Fellowship, and its accompanying outreach.

I was so fascinated by Rice and Perkins' story that I immediately purchased their book, *More Than Equals*. I devoured it. Their story deeply moved me and made me think, "Wow, there is hope for this race problem in America after all!" Not only is their book about mending broken relationships between people of different racial backgrounds, but also about coming together to bring positive change to our shared communities. That fall, I had begun attending a small group Bible study that my roommate Victor was co-leading with his friend Xuan-Vu, a tiny energetic Vietnamese American woman. As I got to know her in the Bible study, I was impressed by how much I got to know her as a person and how genuinely affirming she was of me. She would affectionately call me by my middle name, "Simon." She was a very real person and seemed free of needing to put up any front. It was in that Bible study that we read the gospel of

Matthew and I started to learn about Jesus. It was the first time that I had learned anything about Jesus.

I heard through my small group Bible study that the Christian Fellowship was planning a January break trip to Jackson, Mississippi, to spend time with Rice and Perkins at Voice of Calvary Fellowship and Voice of Calvary Ministries and to see firsthand some of the work they had been doing in the neighborhood. Growing up, I was not a person to take risks, but something inside of me jumped at the opportunity to go on this trip even though I was not a Christian. I signed up.

That week and a half was filled with rich moments. Before we arrived in Jackson, we stopped at the Birmingham Civil Rights Institute to learn more about the history of the Civil Rights Movement. This was the first time that I felt that I learned anything meaningful about the Civil Rights Movement and recognized that people lost their lives and fought for their freedom only a few decades ago. I don't remember spending any significant time on the Civil Rights Movement in my AP U.S. History class in high school. At the museum, I sensed the history of the city and how blacks had fought a long hard battle for their rights and the rights of all Americans. I also sensed that the strength that it took to endure the hardships they faced had a lot to do with their Christian faith. It would otherwise be impossible to persevere nonviolently in the face of that much suffering. I wrote in my journal:

> Seeing the civil rights movement from where it started (down South) was powerful and moving. The presentation of the material — when you first walk in, you are confronted by the "white" and "colored" drinking fountains, the next exhibit with the Klu Klux Klan outfit and the voices and images, the outlines of the movement — the faces, the people, the struggles...Rev. Fred Shuttlesworth, the Freedom Riders, Rev. Martin Luther King Jr...if we are wrong, the Constitution is wrong; if the Constitution is wrong, then God Almighty is wrong. Fighting against injustice...imagine yourself in the position they were in, would you die for a cause? Amazing perseverance...

Throughout the week or so in Jackson, we were fully welcomed and integrated into the Antioch[3] community as if we were just an extended part of the family. I noted in my journal, "immediately I feel the genuine warmth inside the house between the families and for us as people willing to learn." I felt privileged to hear so many peoples' stories almost every evening. We saw the corner that we had heard and read about that had been transformed from drug house to community health center. We lived in the house next door to Antioch and shared meals with the Rice and Perkins' families. As I heard their families speak about how they enjoyed living together because their children had the opportunity to become friends across racial lines, I was moved. In my journal, I commented, "I think the big winners in all this are the kids — the environment they live in and the other playmates they have from the other families. As a result of their parents' decisions, they will grow up more curious and more understanding of the world they live in." I also came to understand that the ideal of the truly interracial church, Voice of Calvary, had not happened overnight, that it had not been an easy process, and that it was still a work in progress. It involved intense commitment to one another and perseverance through painful and hard times. I also learned that living in the city involved a cost as the families talked about the times that their homes had been broken into and how they struggled to remain safe yet still be generous to their neighbors. The idealistic vision I had of living and working in the inner city was being challenged by reality.

However, everywhere we went and in all the people we talked to, I sensed something deeply positive happening. I felt honored to share meals with the Rice and Perkins families and to play with their children. The service work we did was hard, but rewarding. We painted over the dull light blue color of the exterior of the building we stayed in with a warm

---

3 Editor's note: Antioch was the intentional, multiracial, Christian community where Spencer Perkins and Chris Rice, along with their families and several other families, lived together for twelve years.

light tan. During this time of painting and bonding, I saw what a difference having Christ inside of these people called Christians made in their lives. Working and living with people 24-7 means that you see both the good and bad sides to them. Xuan-Vu came on the trip and I grew in admiration of her and how real and authentic she was. I learned that being a Christian doesn't mean you are perfect or that you are happy all the time. I wrote in my journal about Xuan-Vu, "If I could pick the one person who is most honest, open and transparent about her emotions and life it has to be Xuan-Vu." I sensed that her faith as a Christian enabled her to live her life in this way.

A month after the trip, after all that I had seen and witnessed and all I had learned about Jesus from the Bible studies and what the Bible said about issues of justice, I decided to become a Christian. When I joined my friend Victor's Bible study, I was struck by a story called the Parable of the Good Samaritan in the book of Luke. In this story, Jesus tells an expert in the Law the story of a man who was robbed, stripped of his clothes, beaten and left half-dead. Ironically, those who should have been this man's allies and come to his rescue, a priest and a Levite, chose to pass him by. Luke records Jesus saying that each "passed by on the other side." Instead, the one least likely to help, a Samaritan, came to and cared for him, bandaged his wounds, placed the man on his donkey and took him to an inn where he paid for his stay. At the end of his story, Jesus' instructions to this expert in the Law were to "go and do likewise." Another passage in the gospel of John struck me at the time. In John 15:12 Jesus says "My command is this: Love each other as I have loved you." Together these two passages challenge Christians today to live out the gospel as concretely as Jesus described. In a 1963 speech at Western Michigan University the Reverend Dr. Martin Luther King, Jr. spoke of what many of those who are not Christian give as a reason for why they do not become Christians:

The first way that the church can repent, the first way that it can move out into the arena of social reform is to remove the yoke of segregation from its own body....Now that the mistake of the past has been made, I think that the opportunity of the future is to really go out and to transform American society, and where else is there a better place than in the institution that should serve as the moral guardian of the community. The institution that should preach brotherhood and make it a reality within its own body (King 1963).

My experiences in a multiethnic fellowship in college had a direct impact on my subsequent life decisions. I eventually moved to Boston to become part of an Asian American couple's vision to live in Dorchester, an inner-city mostly African American community, and have an impact on it through neighborhood ministry similar to that of Voice of Cavalry. I attended a multiethnic church in Cambridge that was predominantly Asian American and became part of their church planting team in the neighborhood I lived in. Although the church plant did not materialize, I put down roots in Dorchester and became a middle school Humanities teacher in the Boston Public Schools, fulfilling the educational fire inside of me. I hope to be part of the school reform and change effort in Boston, having recently received my license to become a principal. For now, I'm content in the classroom. I attend a small home-based multiethnic, multigenerational church called The Gathering Christian Fellowship. I really can't imagine going to a church that is heavily one race or ethnicity. It just doesn't feel right.

Recently, my friend Mako and I started a spiritual discussion group focussed on figuring out how we can make a difference to life in Dorchester. One member, T, does not believe in the resurrection. His first question to us was "What is the connection between Christian faith and social justice?" He did not see a connection. Perhaps if more Christians lived out Jesus' words in their lives, we would see churches become more reflective of the diversity of our nation and the world. Of course, this diversity must be deep and authentic rather than merely superficial and token. When those

who are not Christians see more diverse churches they may choose to follow Jesus and the Christian faith. They may be like me, and like T. We were
looking for evidence, something we could see, that the Bible these Christians read actually makes a difference in the way that they live.

4

WHITE PEOPLE WORSHIP?

REVEREND YOLANDA DENSON LEHMAN
WITH ALEXIS SPENCER-BYERS

I didn't arrive at Amherst College intentionally. In July of 1998, I married a man who happened to be pursuing a doctoral degree at the University of Massachusetts, Amherst. We began attending the nearest African Methodist Episcopal (AME) Zion Church, Goodwin Memorial, which happens to be across the street from the Cadigan Center, where Paul Sorrentino's office is located. Goodwin's senior pastor, the Reverend Kenneth Lewis, often had dealings with Paul. When I needed a field study assignment during the second year of my Masters in Divinity program at Harvard University, the pastor suggested that I speak to Paul about working with Amherst Christian Fellowship. I did so and was welcomed with open arms. I was grateful that I would be able to do my field study so close to home, and I also looked forward to the opportunity to use my administrative and ministerial gifts. In addition, Paul had led me to believe that perhaps my experience in the Black Church tradition would be an asset.

The first time I attended an Amherst Christian Fellowship large group meeting, I was shocked—and that's putting it mildly! The Fellowship's worship was a foreign experience to me.

When I was born, I went almost straight from my mother's womb to the church nursery. The Missionary Baptist Church in St. Louis that my family attended was like a second womb. It nourished me and kept me safe until I was ready to venture out into the larger world. Several other children were born into the church around the same time I was, and we grew up together, learning to sing, dance, speak publicly, and develop leadership skills. Throughout most of my youth, we went to school and went to church. That was it. That was our life.

Our church was 100 percent African-American[4] and very traditional. We sang spirituals, gospel songs, and the occasional anthem. We had fiery preachers who proclaimed the Gospel with vigor and energy, and congregations who helped by "talking back." I can't recall ever seeing a white person at my home church growing up. One aspect of the worship that I remember particularly was the "moaning" that took place at the beginning of the service. The Deacons of the church (all male in those years) would stand in front of the congregation, and one of them, often an elderly gentleman, would moan something like, "I love the Lord, He heard my cry." The other Deacons, along with the rest of the worshippers, would respond with the same words, drawn out over many, many syllables and tones. It took forever! I remember being told that the reason we did this was because "the devil can't understand you if you moan." I also remember, as a child, thinking the whole thing was insane. "What were they doing, and why was it taking so long?"

As I grew older and I experienced trials, tribulations, worries, and fears of my own, I began to understand and appreciate the value of moaning—a tradition that harkens back to the hardships of slavery. Today, I often moan with my daughter: I call, and she responds. It is a tradition that I am proud to pass down to another generation.

During my childhood, my parents intentionally educated me about African-American history. My father was the publisher of the St. Louis Black Pages, and he drilled into us the importance of black heritage and black history. My mother supplemented his teaching on Black Power with

4 Editor's note: Ethnic terms, such as African American, can properly be hyphenated or non-hyphenated. While most contributors have chosen not to hyphenate in this book, Yolanda is taking legitimate exception to this because she feels strongly that hyphenation is a way to join her two identities.

knowledge regarding how our faith had sustained our people, particularly during slavery and the civil rights movement era. I was steeped in African-American culture and tradition, and I still treasure that nurture and exposure. As an African-American family, we were proud of who we were, and we held our heads high.

This was particularly important because my parents chose to live in "the county," the suburbs of St. Louis, so my sister and I grew up in a predominantly white neighborhood and attended predominantly white schools. As a result, I always felt that I existed in a place "betwixt and between." I didn't quite belong in either culture. Obviously, I wasn't white. But many in the black community considered me an "Oreo"—black on the outside and white on the inside. Church was a refuge for me, for it was one of the only places where I was known and valued for who I was.

As a teenager, I began to do my own reading about slavery, and I learned some very disturbing things. I learned that many white "Christians" had used the Bible to justify the practice. From that information, I developed a sense that white Christians didn't really understand the Bible, and that they were not very good at loving God and loving their neighbors. I figured that a group that had misused the Bible in the past would likely also misuse it in the present. In light of the racism I'd witnessed and experienced in my white community and schools, and because I didn't know any white Christians well enough to visit their churches, I was pretty much convinced that white Christians were not to be trusted. My church continued to be my oasis. It was the place I went to escape the white culture of power, where I could see African-American people in leadership and be with others who shared and celebrated my heritage.

In college I joined the AME Zion Church, part of a historically black denomination that is more than 200 years old. It had the same feel and flavor of my home church and I began my teaching and preaching ministry there. Over the years, I had many white friends, but I can't say that I was ever intentionally involved in racial reconciliation, and I had never before worshipped in a non-black environment. The closest I had come was hearing "white" contemporary worship music on the Christian radio station as a teenager.

And there I was, at my first Amherst Christian Fellowship meeting. The room seemed extremely white to me, even though there were some Asian American and African-American students in attendance. The music was terribly dissonant to my ears. I had never heard songs like "Open the Eyes of My Heart" or "Lord I Lift Your Name on High." I could not understand why they sang each verse only once and why there were no percussion instruments. Why did no one seem to be singing out? Why was everyone silent during the "sermon"? I was amazed by the fact that no one clapped or shouted, "Hallelujah!" I spent that first meeting sitting in my chair, thinking, "This isn't right! Don't they know you're supposed to...fill in the blank...?" My thoughts progressed from there to: "These poor white Christians! They just don't know how to worship..."

For a season, worshiping with Amherst Christian Fellowship remained a totally foreign experience. The first time I heard the Fellowship sing "Amazing Grace," one of the best-loved hymns of many black and white congregations, I honestly didn't know what song it was. No lyrics were displayed, and the rhythm and speed were so different from the version I had grown up with, that it took some time for my brain to register that it was a song I knew.

As the shock of my first experiences began to wear off, God came at me from several fronts, challenging me to think in new ways about non-black Christians and about unity in God's Body. Although I initially found Amherst Christian Fellowship's praise and worship style disorienting and even unpleasant, I immediately recognized that the group was a warm and wel-

coming fellowship, open to new ideas and practices and teaching strong
biblical doctrine. Although they probably found me a bit quirky, I was accepted, and I appreciated that. I began to study the Scriptures through the
lens of racial reconciliation. As I did that, it occurred to me that if I disliked
multiethnic fellowship, I was going to hate heaven! I saw the multiethnic
fellowship of the early Christians in Acts 2, and I saw the vision of John in
Revelation 7:9. It began to be very important to me that I learn to worship
with folks who were red, yellow, black, and yes, even white—for the sake
of the Gospel. I learned that all of God's children are precious and capable
of great love, great light, and great ministry.

I also read Spencer Perkins and Chris Rice's *More Than Equals* during that
season, and their book helped me to develop the language, theology, and
Bible-based knowledge with which to articulate my visceral – heart and
soul and gut — understanding of the truth.

The bulk of my journey toward a passionate commitment to bridging
the ethnic divide in The Church came through personal relationships—my
friendships with Paul and his wife, Karen, and my interactions with several
Amherst Christian Fellowship students.

While I was with the Fellowship, I interacted with students on many
levels—counseling, participating in small group Bible studies, and praying one-on-one and in groups. Students walked with me throughout my
first pregnancy; several of my students were among the first to hold my
baby outside of the hospital. As we shared our lives in these very deep
and meaningful ways, I realized that they were every bit as Christian as
I was. If we could play, ponder, and pray together, surely we could worship together! One of these students, a European American young woman
named Brooke, proved the point. Brooke worshipped at my AME Zion
church while she was a student at Amherst. She was one of a handful of
white people who attended that church, and she wasn't just warming a

pew cross-culturally; Brooke put her heart and soul into worshipping with her African-American brothers and sisters. I found her example inspiring. We continue to be friends to this day.

I also found the example of Paul and Karen Sorrentino extremely influential in my growth as a reconciler. Paul is like a pit bull when it comes to reconciliation and multiethnic worship. He just doesn't let the thing go. No matter what kind of event or activity we were planning, he was always thinking about how to include students of color. I quickly realized that since Paul was so committed to multiethnic fellowship, I was going to have to get on board or jump ship. His commitment, conviction, and "stick-to-it-ness" were contagious.

Paul's wife, Karen, was equally committed. Karen has an incredible gift of hospitality. As there were always students of many different ethnicities and cultures in her home, she had many opportunities to consistently find ways to build bridges, to welcome people as she would welcome Christ, and to create peace, harmony, and a sense of "home" for whoever was there. Karen absolutely refused to allow anyone who was in her presence to be—or feel—unheard, unseen, or unimportant. I was, and am, and always will be inspired by her gift and her intentional practice of that gift. She is a role model and mentor for me. Since leaving Amherst, I have been committed to trying to recreate the feeling I had in the Sorrentino home for all of the people who enter my home or local church. For many of us, Karen was the hands, feet, and smile of Jesus in our lives! I can only prayerfully and humbly strive to follow her example as I love and serve those who are different from me.

These dear friends impressed me by their commitment to creating multiethnic fellowship for the sake of the Gospel, even though it meant frequently stepping out of their comfort zones and taking risks. Prior to Amherst Christian Fellowship, I looked on all white people with suspicion. I figured they were "guilty until proven innocent." But my involvement with the Sorrentinos and the students at Amherst Christian Fellowship changed all that. It made me totally committed to living out a Biblical standard: Love God, and love neighbor as self. I am convinced that my neighbors are all of God's children, regardless of race, ethnicity, or culture.

My tenure with Amherst Christian Fellowship provided many valuable life lessons, but one that was especially significant for me is the understanding that there are manifold legitimate ways to worship. I eventually came to the conclusion that worship in the African-American tradition is great, but so is worship in the European American tradition, including Vineyard-style songs. I can honestly say that I now love songs like "Open the Eyes of My Heart." I sing them, I listen to them on the radio regularly, and I don't feel out of place in fellowships that sing this music. It was beautiful—and radical—to discover that I could hear and feel God through different songs and traditions. When I finally stopped fighting the worship style of Amherst Christian Fellowship and allowed myself to practice a "blending" of the styles, I found a deepness and richness to my faith experience that I hadn't had before.

Because reconciliation is a two-way street, I am happy to report that I wasn't the only one who was changing. The biggest changes occurred around worship. While I was there, African-Americans really stepped up to the plate to help lead worship. We began to sing spirituals and Gospel music. I remember teaching the fellowship the importance of learning to clap on the second and fourth beats, rather than the first and third, when we were singing Gospel music. People raised in the Black Church just know this. It is "natural." I had never heard clapping on one and three until I started worshipping with white people. I remember the fellowship members really, really struggling to go against what was natural to them in order to do what was natural for the African-American students. That touched my heart, and it was a fun time as well. In addition to clapping, we began to teach the students that it was all right to lift their hands, to shout for joy, to laugh and sing loud. I even got the students to say "Amen!" once in a while when I was preaching at Friday Night Fellowship.

And then there was the ongoing "Amazing Grace" story. Generally, in my experience, when white people sing Amazing Grace, it is fast and measured, as it was the first time I heard it at Amherst Christian Fellowship. By contrast, when African-Americans sing it, it is very, very, very slow, unmeasured, and soulful. I remember teaching our way to the Fellowship and thinking they would never understand. But, one day, we sang it "right"—that is to say, in the style familiar to me. It was the most spiritual moment of my time at Amherst Christian Fellowship. I felt the Holy Spirit come into the room as we sang, all in one accord, the song that for many black Christians is the most significant song in our repertoire. It was an awesome and life-changing experience, and it proved to me that multiethnic fellowship can work, if everyone gives a little and takes a little.

As these changes were occurring in Amherst Christian Fellowship, we began to see an increase in the regular attendance of African-American and Asian American students. This growth in minority participation in the fellowship was personally encouraging to me, and it also underscored the importance of being intentional about diversity in the fellowship. There were students of color on campus who were looking for a place to come together with other Christians—they just needed to see evidence that they would be welcome, and their traditions valued, in that place.

Since leaving Amherst Christian Fellowship, I have continued to worship in multiethnic fellowships. It just makes sense to me. When I think about the fact that Sunday morning is the most segregated day of the week in America, it makes me sad; I'm sure it grieves the heart of God. Currently, my family and I worship at Atonement Lutheran Church in St. Cloud, Minnesota. I am one of the pastors in this predominantly white congregation of

Christians. If someone had asked me twelve years ago if I thought I would ever offer pastoral leadership to a church of 1,600 European Americans, I would have answered with a resounding, "No!" But, God has a sense of humor and a way of constantly pushing our boundaries and challenging us to prove that we will actually act upon what we profess to believe.

I was called to Atonement for many reasons; but one of the most compelling, for me, was their expressed desire to become a more multiethnic fellowship. When Atonement was created fifty years ago, the neighborhood was largely white. Now, the neighborhood around the church is changing; in fact, our city is changing. Atonement has a desire to change with the community and a desire to minister to the needs of all of God's children.

In the years ahead, the Atonement Church family will prayerfully implement many of the lessons I learned during my tenure with Amherst Christian Fellowship. This is a big challenge, but I serve a big God! Where else can I truly see if the principles of racial reconciliation will work than in a denomination that is 97 percent white, the Evangelical Lutheran Church in America, and in a church that is whiter than that? These are exciting times. I am thrilled by the challenge before me, but I must also be honest enough to admit that there are some things that I grieve for as well.

As much as I love worshiping with believers of other races, and as compelling as I find the vision of multiethnic fellowship, there are things I miss from my Black Church background. I miss the beat and flavor of the songs I grew up with. I miss a charismatic and gregarious worship experience— lifting hands, stomping feet, playing tambourines, shouting hallelujah, and talking to the pastor as she preaches. I miss the beauty of church attire, men in suits and women in fancy hats, suits, and heels. I especially miss the patience that African-Americans have in worship. We are unafraid to worship two or three hours at a time, while in the predominantly white churches, sixty minutes tends to be the norm.

Sometimes, I feel like to make a multiethnic fellowship work, we go to the "lowest common denominator." In an effort to diversify a predominantly white worshipping community, we are tempted to focus our efforts on making the least number of white people uncomfortable rather than boldly welcoming the variety of worship elements and styles that will make our new neighbors of different ethnic backgrounds comfortable as well. Perhaps our goal should be to initially make everyone uncomfortable as we seek to blend our traditions into one cohesive whole that is comfortable, yet challenging, for all. Finally, I must confess that I am also grieving the loss of the "Black Church experience" in the lives of my children. I wonder how they will be affected by the absence of a place where they can consistently be around other black people in worship, and specifically around Christian adults who are able to help them understand themselves in a still very white and very racist country. I worry that I may be cheating my babies by not giving them a "100 percent authentic" African-American church experience. I fear that they will lose touch with their ethnic heritage—with the spirituals and hymns that sustained our people during the long years of slavery and Jim Crow segregation, and with the rich prayer tradition upon which African-American Christians have depended for hundreds of years. I fret that they will not have the spiritual grounding that they will need the first time someone calls them the "N Word" or that they won't have the fortitude to stand firm when they encounter racism from outside—or inside—of The Church.

Having confessed these fears, which I view as wholly legitimate, I am absolutely convinced that the sacrifices are worth making. I don't choose multiethnic worship because it is the most comfortable option for me; I choose it because I believe it represents God's best-case scenario for God's children. Multiethnic worship reflects, albeit imperfectly, the eternal reality of Heaven. When I've tried to go back—when I've visited AME Zion or other all-black congregations—I feel a strong sense of dissonance. It just feels like there's something—or rather, someone—missing from the picture. I feel out of place, like once again I'm "betwixt and between" two worlds. I love the tradition and style of the African-American church. I love the liberation theology that teaches that our Christian faith has everything to do with bringing about social, economic, and political justice for all of God's children, and I agree with the Scriptural interpretation on most issues. I just find that I'm no longer satisfied trying to worship God without brothers and sisters of other ethnic backgrounds.

From time to time, I attempt to share my passion for multiethnic fellowship with other African-American pastors. They are often very open to the idea—in theory. Of course, non-black people are welcome at their worship services! But unless we are intentional, our practice tends not to match our theory. Unless we make an effort to include people, and elements, of diverse backgrounds in our services, ethnically different visitors are going to peek through the door, see that no one in the sanctuary looks like them, and head to the church down the street where they feel more safe and comfortable.

Despite the sometimes slow progress of black and white churches toward racial reconciliation, my own life experience gives me hope. So do the examples of many people that I've known, both in Amherst Christian Fellowship and in the St. Cloud community.

Until recently, I taught a course entitled "Race in America" at the local university. During my tenure, I found that I spent the majority of my time convincing my predominantly white students that racism does, in fact, remain a problem in America in the twenty-first century. In fact, I would spend the first third of every semester helping students to wrestle with the question, "Is racism real?" We would spend the second third of the semester answering the question, "Is white privilege real?" Then we would spend the final third of the semester "acting out": encouraging white students to find ways to activate their privilege on behalf of—and in cooperation with—people of color in order to create a more just, fair, and equitable society for all.

It encourages me greatly that about 90 percent of my students, the same percentage as those who didn't initially believe racism was a problem, left the course committed to doing the hard work of being actively anti-rac-ist—a concept I introduce to my students using Beverly Daniel Tatum's 1997 book, *Why Are All the Black Kids Sitting Together in the Cafeteria?* What gives me even greater joy is the fact that the church was often a part of the process for many of my students. During the course, students engaged in a "field study" assignment. They went to a location where they would be an ethnic minority. Since most of my students were Christian, many chose to attend a church made up of people who did not share their ethnic heri-tage. It gave me tremendous joy when my students came back from this assignment saying things like, "I felt so alive. I can't wait to go back! I was welcomed so warmly!" It was often this experience of multiethnic worship that changed their lives in powerful ways and motivated them to commit themselves to working for racial justice.

And that is as it should be. The Church of Jesus Christ should be leading the way toward a more loving, just, and equitable society. We should be the ones setting an example—in word and deed—of how to love across race, ethnicity, color, national origin, language, culture, or any other defin-ing characteristic. It is up to us, as Christians, to offer a viable alternative to the segregationist activities in our country and world. And if we fail to offer leadership in this most critical arena, it's not just those watching us who will suffer. We ourselves will miss out on the richness and diversity of our manifold ethnicities and cultures, and we will forfeit the precious gift that multiethnic worship is to The Church, the world, and all of God's creation. This must never be so; we are better than this.

People often ask, "What would Jesus do?" We already know the answer. Jesus drew Jews and Gentiles, men and women, adults and children, healthy and sick, rich and poor into the circle of His love. If Jesus were to build a local church today, it would probably be the most diverse body of human beings on the planet! As followers of Christ we can—we must— follow His example. This is the essence of the Good News message: God is love. We must love all of God's children as we welcome them to worship our Lord and Savior Jesus Christ, who lived, and died, and lived again that we might experience the fullness of joy that comes from living as a forgiven people set free to love God, and to love our neighbors as ourselves. Amen! May it be so, Lord!

5

WE ARE ALL ADVANTAGED

PAUL WHITING

From my first moments on the Amherst College campus, I was struck by the incredible diversity of our incoming class. Of eighteen students at the first floor meeting for our dorm, four were Asian American, four Latino, five black, and five white. I had never experienced this kind of diversity in my Orange County neighborhood. The diversity of the Amherst College community would be a permanent and defining feature of my college experience. It would challenge me to confront my identity as a white person and to understand how this portion of my identity had contributed to my perspective on campus ministry.

I was also struck that first day by the level of talent and accomplishment among my classmates. At our first class meeting, the Dean of Students gave us his "best & brightest" speech. We were, he said, the most talented, accomplished, and ethnicly diverse class Amherst had ever welcomed. Despite mutterings around me of "that's probably not true," or "they say that every year," I soon found reason to believe the Dean. My classmates were talented and experienced across a broad range of interests and activities. The student body at Amherst seemed to me to be uniformly privileged. Amherst students had remarkable God-given talents and abilities. They also seemed to have the opportunities and resources necessary to develop these talents substantially. Despite the racial, ethnic, and geographic diversity of our class, almost everyone I met seemed to have grown up in privileged circumstances like mine. This conclusion, drawn by the end of my first week on campus, would be challenged through my involvement with the Amherst Christian Fellowship as I confronted the assumptions that had led me to make it.

In the middle of my sophomore year, I was asked to join the Amherst Christian Fellowship leadership team. One of our first assignments was to read an article by our staff worker, Paul Sorrentino. The article introduced the theory and practice that had made Amherst Christian Fellowship a thriving multiethnic fellowship. I had enjoyed the multiethnic character of the Fellowship so much that I was surprised to find myself unsettled by Paul's paper.

When we met to discuss the paper, I shared openly that I was unsettled. We spent the rest of the meeting trying to understand where these emotions were coming from. One possible answer was that the paper brought into sharp focus an issue I had been working on in my own personal faith journey. I had been growing to understand that God was more concerned with the attitude of one's heart than He was with the number and kind of Christian activities one performed. Paul's paper spoke directly to this point, exposing the implicit message often communicated within Christian organizations that one's commitment to Christ could be determined by one's involvement in the Christian fellowship or church. Often the more activities a person does with the fellowship, the more spiritual he or she is assumed to be. This was exactly the perspective I had held until earlier that year, and God was in the process of transforming my mind to think differently. But after reading Paul's article, something inside me caused me to revert back to my old way of thinking – that doing more ministry was better and was more spiritual. Paul's paper served as a litmus test to determine whether or not I had truly learned this important lesson God had been teaching me throughout the year. Sobering as it was, my reaction to the article revealed that I hadn't; I was still clearly a "work in progress."

Another idea introduced in Paul's paper that left me even more unsettled was Carl Ellis' concept of "core issues." Ellis argues that each individual
faces three types of core issues: personal, social, and cultural. Paul's paper
applied this concept to involvement in campus ministry activities. For majority students, most social and cultural core issues are met by the broader
society, leaving these students free to spend time and energy focusing on
personal core issues. Since the social and cultural core issues of minority
students often remain unmet by society, such students might choose to become involved in groups and activities that address these categories of core
issues, which often relate centrally to these students' identities. This becomes a problem when minority students are forced to reduce or give up
their involvement in other activities in order to become more involved in
a Christian fellowship group. Ultimately, when students experience these
conflicting expectations, they may be forced to make fundamental loyalty
decisions about where they will invest their time. Minority students often feel that, in making these decisions, they are essentially answering the
question, "Am I Hispanic American / African American / Asian American or
am I Christian?" Consequently, Paul argued, fellowships must make a con-
certed effort to avoid placing minority students in this position.

I found the idea of core issues interesting. I had never, that I could remember, thought about my own core issues. As a white person, many of
mine had been met by society at large. But I was very hesitant to apply this
understanding of core issues to Amherst College students and the Amherst
Christian Fellowship. At our leadership team meeting, I remember rattling
off arguments against the core issues concept and reasons why it did not
apply at Amherst. As a white person it made me feel as if I would have to
do even more than my minority brothers and sisters in order to be seen as
making the fellowship a priority. I was unsettled by the fact that this paper
seemed to be giving minority students an "excuse" for reduced involvement in the campus fellowship.

What I reacted most strongly against was the assumption that minority students could be lumped together and that anything could be said about the core issues of any particular minority group on the Amherst College campus. I resisted the application of the core issues concept to the Fellowship because I seriously doubted whether minority students at Amherst had indeed suffered from unmet core issues the same way minority students in general had. At Amherst the "rules didn't apply "and minority students at Amherst didn't fit the "mold" of the typical minority student.

My point of view followed directly from my understanding of racial diversity at Amherst formed during my first few days on campus. While racial and ethnic diversity was extraordinarily evident, I understood this diversity in the context of our common identity as Amherst students, the "best and the brightest." The fellow students I had come to know during the first half of my college experience, had made it to Amherst in part because their core issues had been met. In general, I felt that most of my classmates, even minority students, had come from families which were at least equally and often more stable financially than mine.

As I left the meeting, I felt even more unsettled than when I had arrived. But by God's grace, over the next several months, God kept reminding me of those critical lessons He had been patiently teaching me all year. He desired an intimate relationship with me, and He was concerned more with the attitude of my heart as I performed my various church and ministry activities than with the activities themselves. Over time, by reaffirming and deepening my understanding of these important lessons, God brought completion to a work He had begun at the beginning of the year. This transformation in my perspective toward my own ministry activities helped to overcome some of the resistance I had felt toward Paul's paper. I now understood that an African American believer who felt led to invest herself in the Black Student Union could bring as much glory to God as I could by serving on the leadership team and leading a Bible study for athletes. God would delight equally in the Asian American student who committed himself to serving the other members of the Asian Culture House as an act of worship, the Latino student who felt called to serve his class on the student council, and the white student who led praise and worship at his local church. What really mattered was that these activities were pursued prayerfully, obediently, and with an attitude of worship.

God also began to transform my perspective of racial and ethnic inequalities. After reading Paul's article on multiethnic ministry, I had concluded that such inequalities were not significant among the Amherst student body, the only diverse population I had encountered firsthand. From that point forward, however, God began to teach me quite convincingly that inequalities do exist; they exist in Western Massachusetts, in the United States, and around the world. And more importantly, He began to provide me with opportunities to respond obediently.

God used several courses during my junior year to open my eyes to the reality of racial inequalities in America. One such course was called "Reading, Writing, and Teaching," an English course studying education and pedagogy. Jonathan Kozol's *Savage Inequalities* – which revealed the abysmal condition of public education in America's poorest urban communities—had a particularly strong impact on me. The course also involved a weekly teaching assignment at Holyoke High School, less than a half an hour from Amherst. Formerly a bustling and prosperous paper mill town, Holyoke experienced a post-industrial decline and has become economically depressed in recent decades. The school is inadequately funded and lacks the technology and other resources necessary to provide the quality of education offered at public schools in more prosperous suburban communities. As a result, the student body of Holyoke High, the vast majority of whom are students of color, experience the reality of educational inequalities every day, just as did the students in Kozol's study.

Another course that influenced my thinking was "The Weary Blues: Mourning and Loss in African American Literature and Culture." We studied how African Americans have dealt with the realities of mourning and loss unique to their experience in the United States and have found expression for these painful emotions in literary genres ranging from plays to poetry to hip-hop music. What most struck me about the literature we read in the course wasn't the means by which African Americans have expressed their experiences; rather, it was the fact that the African American experience has, with few exceptions, been an experience characterized by mourning and loss. This was a difficult realization for me! But when the course ended, I found myself drawn to the African American experience all the more — so much so that I decided to pursue an independent study project with the same professor the following semester. She guided me through important literature from the decades leading up to and including the Civil Rights Movement, and we met weekly to discuss these readings. She served as a sounding board for me to confront and process the wide range of emotions that were evoked in me as I read this literature. As I entered my senior year, God was softening my heart, transforming my mind, and clarifying my understanding of racial inequalities.

That December I joined the sizeable, multiethnic delegation representing the Amherst Christian Fellowship at the Urbana '03 student missions convention. The previous summer I had prayerfully decided to take a "year off" between college and medical school, and I came to Urbana wondering if I would get a sense from God about what I should do during that year. At Urbana I decided to attend a seminar entitled "Taking the Plunge: Short-Term Urban Ministry Options." At the beginning of the seminar, before he began teaching about urban issues, the facilitator asked us to take a few minutes to pray and think about how God might have already been preparing us for urban ministry. In those next few moments, my mind was quickly flooded with examples of how God had used all kinds of experiences to prepare me to serve in an urban setting - my family background as the son and grandson of career public school teachers, a missions trip I had taken to a poor city in Mexico, many college courses, including a brand new course in U.S. urban history I would be taking during my final semester.

It was remarkable to recognize in retrospect how God had been preparing me to serve Him in urban ministry – intellectually through my college courses, relationally through my experiences on a diverse college campus, and spiritually through my involvement with a vibrant multiethnic campus ministry. Having heard God's voice so clearly, I was eager to find an opportunity to pursue this calling during the year following graduation. Before I left Urbana, I canvassed the exhibition hall searching high and low among the hundreds of missions organizations for urban ministry opportunities I could pursue. Ideally, I hoped to find an opportunity to do urban ministry in Houston, where Gloria, my future wife, was a student at Rice University. We felt that being in the same city would help our relationship to grow as we moved toward engagement and ultimately marriage.

Although I did not find any opportunities at Urbana, on my flight back home to Los Angeles, I actually met a woman who worked for an urban ministry organization with multiple sites across the country, including one in Houston. As soon as I arrived home, I visited the organization's website and was thrilled to learn about a position available at the Houston site the following January – exactly when I would be available to start. I couldn't believe it! Three days after revealing my heart for urban ministry, God provided me with a perfect opportunity to serve in urban ministry in Houston.

The Center for Student Missions in Houston hosts groups of junior high, high school, and college students on short-term urban service projects. The Center's role is to connect these groups with local community service agencies throughout the city, providing opportunities for students to understand more about the urban experience through service. Working alongside these groups transformed my understanding of racial and ethnic inequalities, particularly as they are made manifest in the inner city. I tutored elementary school students who attended schools like those described in the sociology books I had read. I learned of the struggles that face homeless individuals and families and the barriers that prevent them from re-establishing economic stability. I gained a better understanding of the social and political forces that contribute to the geographic and socio-economic marginalization of the urban poor. And I experienced living in the inner city for the first time – understanding what it feels like to stand out in public based on the color of my skin. In Houston, the Center for Student Missions partnered with the I Corinthians 13 Church, a local inner-city church that provides housing for the visiting groups and for seasonal Center for Student Missions staff like me. The partnership with this African American congregation and its youth outreach program provided me with an invaluable opportunity to work side-by-side and across racial boundaries. I was blessed by new friendships with the church's youth ministry interns, Reginald and Willie-Earl. I lived with these young men, who had grown up in the neighborhood themselves and were blessed by the ministry of this church when they were younger.

One of the highlights of working at the Center for Student Missions was seeing God at work in the hearts of the junior high and high school students we hosted. Having traveled to Houston primarily from more affluent, less racially diverse communities throughout Texas and the neighboring states, most of these students were unfamiliar with the inner city and individuals of different ethnicities. It was beautiful to see these students mature over the course of the week they spent with us, overcoming some of their initial fears and uneasiness toward people different from themselves. During the week, students had ample opportunities to demonstrate genuine acts of love through service. Stereotypes were broken down and students were transformed.

Often the most meaningful experience for our students was the chance to worship at a vibrant inner-city African American church in downtown Houston. It was clear that many students had never been to a church with non-whites before, and most of them had never worshiped in the exuberant, animated style that characterized this church's musical worship. As white students, the experience of worshiping in a predominately African American congregation gave them a glimpse of multiethnic ministry in the church setting, and this was something they embraced and enjoyed thoroughly. Countless students commented that this experience was the most memorable portion of their entire trip. The more informal ministry times at our host church also had a tremendous impact on our students, as they spent time with the inner-city youth and youth leaders who were involved in the church's ministry program. Many students reported their time spent with the neighborhood kids as being their most significant experience of the trip.

The experience of multiethnic worship and multiethnic community ministry had a profound impact not only on our students, but also on me. Considering the breadth of service experiences our students had over the course of their week in Houston, the fact that these glimpses of multiethnic ministry had so significantly influenced our students reaffirmed what I had learned at Amherst – multiethnic ministry can be powerful and transformative.

While I was working at the Center for Student Missions, my fiancé Gloria was also in a process of recognizing the value of multiethnic ministry, especially in the local church setting. She had attended a predominately white Baptist church in a relatively affluent Houston neighborhood during her first two years at Rice. But after returning from a semester abroad in

Chile, where for the first time she experienced the blessing of corporate worship with believers of different ethnicities, she sought out a multiethnic church during her junior year at Rice. Formerly a Chinese congregation with services only in Mandarin, Jireh Bible Church had sensed a call to be intentionally multiethnic and had responded by hiring an African American pastor and starting a second service in English.

By the time I arrived in Houston, Gloria had already been attending for a month. Worshiping together in this diverse body of believers, where we were among a 10% white minority convinced us of the beauty and richness of a multiethnic church body. We benefited tremendously from the sermons offered by both the Chinese American pastor, formerly a mechanical engineer, and the African American pastor, who had previous experience as a family counselor and helped us with pre-marital counseling later that semester. Their diverse backgrounds and prior experience made their sermons replete with practical application of the scriptures to the real-life struggles Christians face. The musical worship was a unique blend of two cultural worship styles, and church potlucks gave members a chance to try and appreciate ethnically diverse foods. Above all, we had the unique opportunity to worship the Lord as people united primarily by our faith in Christ.

More recently, God called us to Boston, where I completed medical school and am currently an orthopaedic surgery resident. Gloria, now my wife, is pursuing a doctorate in history. When looking for a church home, we made it a priority to find one with an ethnically diverse congregation. During medical school, we were happy to find Cambridgeport Baptist Church, a multiethnic and multinational congregation of roughly 200 people. The richness of multiethnic church life was especially apparent when individuals, typically internationals pursuing degrees or doing academic research in the Boston area, would come to faith through relationships with members of our church family. It was the bittersweet moments, when the church prayed for and "sent" these new Christians back to their home nations as messengers of the gospel, that the beauty of multiethnic ministry in the local church was most evident to me. A multiethnic church is perfectly poised to reach non-believing people of all ethnicities, especially in a diverse city such as Boston, where individuals have come from around the world. And as individuals come to faith and are nurtured in the church body, they are equipped and ready to be sent out — whether literally or figuratively — to proclaim the gospel to the ends of the earth, bringing to life the portrait of the throne of God in Revelation 7, when "people of every tribe, tongue, nation, and language," stand before the throne of God in worship.

After moving to a different part of the Boston area for my residency, we have also moved our church home to Park Street Church, an ethnically diverse congregation that similarly emphasizes reaching international scholars and engaging the university campuses in the Boston area with the truth of the gospel. Ultimately, we feel the Lord is calling us to serve Him in the university setting, where we would have opportunities to teach and mentor a diverse group of students and residents in our respective fields. Wherever the Lord leads us in the future, we are committed to joining a multiethnic church, a place we would feel comfortable inviting students of all ethnicities to attend.

Ultimately, I hope to share not only the skills and experience I will gain from my residency training in orthopaedic surgery, but also the healing power of the gospel with the underserved, caring for their physical and spiritual needs. We hope to remain connected to a multiethnic church that would recognize this work as advancing the Kingdom of God and working toward bringing about the Biblical vision of the Church depicted in Revelation 7. Lord willing, may it be so!

6

PAUL & TIMOTHY

REVEREND TIMOTHY JONES

It was a day that I will not forget. After years of studying, praying, serving, and working, it had finally come time for me to be ordained, to be recognized as a minister of the Gospel and to receive the title of "Reverend." How humbling! The way that God orchestrated this day was amazing. When I look back at it now I know that it had to have been by God's Grace and by that Grace alone.

Everything about this day felt natural and blessed. I was in my home church, Pilgrim Journey Baptist Church in Richmond, Virginia. I was surrounded by family and friends, including my parents, both Deacons, and my grandmother, the widow of the church's former pastor, my beloved grandfather. There, as I knelt down in front of the church, with dozens of ministers and deacons, friends and family laying their hands on me to send me off into ministry, the person leading the prayer was my long time mentor and good friend Paul. Our names were a blessed coincidence, bringing to mind another Paul and another Timothy[5]. Paul had known me and mentored me for many years. There really is no one else I would rather have sending me off into formal ministry than this man. The fact that he was the only white man in the church was exceedingly inconsequential to everyone involved.

There were plenty of people who might have served as my mentor. My grandfather had been my pastor for the first 17 years of my life. He was

---

5 One of the great mentoring relationships found in the Bible is between the Apostle Paul and his young protégé Timothy.

an amazing man of God with a wealth of experience built up over his 30 plus years in ministry. We had a strong grandfather-grandson relationship. It is not difficult for me to see that relationship blossoming into an even deeper one. But I received my call to ministry in Massachusetts, far from home, and my grandfather's untimely death made this sort of relationship impossible.

The pastor of the church I attended while in college would have been a fine candidate. He was young, cool, charismatic—the kind of guy that someone like me would love to be around. He has served as the model for my preaching. But his ultra busy schedule prevented him from being the spiritual mentor that most young ministers crave: one that is hands on, genuinely shows that he cares, and puts plenty of time into the relationship. Though he was neither the most "natural pick" nor the "glamour" pick, God gave me the best pick in the Reverend Dr. Paul Sorrentino. Our relationship is proof of the faithfulness of God. Our development as friends has not been an easy road, and there were initially some difficulties presented by our different ethnic backgrounds, but God has walked with us through this process to make this relationship a reality.

Before Paul and I had our first conversation, barriers already separated us. Growing up in the still socially segregated south, I had a negative attitude toward white clergy. Before coming to Amherst, I had never had a conversation with a white minister or pastor. When I thought of white clergy I thought of one of three horrible stereotypes: 1) A boring, "ho hum" preacher who would be terrified if a black person walked into his or her church; 2) A charismatic, prosperity peddling televangelist selling prayer cloths; or 3) A "confess to me, my son" unapproachable Catholic priest in an ornate robe and fancy hat. Worst of all, when I thought of white clergy I often thought of pastors from years past who preached the good news of Jesus Christ but held slaves. I thought of men who could quote the entire

Gospel of Matthew, and then ran the Klan meetings on Sunday evenings. Needless to say, I had little built-in trust of white clergy.

Each of us enters into every relationship with prejudices or biases, with preconceived notions that could be based on little or much fact. We bring all of our history to the table when we begin any relationship. While clearly my prejudices were unfair, they were real. All white clergy are not racist nor do they all lack integrity. But at that particular point in time, it did not matter whether my preconceived notions were based on much fact, little fact, or no fact. They existed and they served as a barrier to any intercultural mentoring I might experience. We each bring "cultural baggage" with us as well. If there has been hurt in the history of two cultures, there is a good chance that this hurt has created lasting pain that serves as a barrier to cross cultural relationships. We cannot assume that making this bond across cultures will be as easy as making bonds within one particular culture.

My first lunch with Paul came at his request. He was one of the first people on campus to contact me at the start of my senior year. He heard through the grapevine that I'd gone through an amazing transformation over the summer and he just wanted to have a conversation. Other leaders in the Christian fellowship had passed on bits and pieces of my story and he wanted to hear about it himself. He felt the need to ask me if I had any questions about ways to serve and he wanted to welcome me into the community of believers on campus.

I entered this first conversation with skepticism: Why would he want to put so much time and effort into me? Why would this man, who barely knew me, be willing to spend one-on-one time with me? Beyond that, would I even be able to open up to him?

Although I hardly knew Paul, one thing lowered the barrier. I had seen him at every African American function on campus in my previous three

years. Amherst College holds a traditional African American styled worship service twice each semester. Though I did not attend church regularly
during my first three years, I attended almost every Bi-Semester service.
Paul was at every Bi-Semester that I attended. He was also at multiple
panel discussions and lectures on issues I was concerned about. While I
was hesitant to meet with this white clergy member, I knew he had made
an effort to experience my culture.

When we met I was immediately taken aback by Paul's humble spirit.
His voice expressed his compassion for me, a young man he was just meeting. The man was obviously a saint. I felt horrified for the preconceived
notions I had come with. This man was white, but he knew Jesus and you
could see that light shining off of him a mile away. I had never trusted white
clergy but I immediately fell in love with the God in this man.

God can help us overcome any and all barriers that exist between brothers and sisters in Christ. Our first task is to simply do our best to portray
the fruit of the Spirit in all of our interactions[6]. Paul led with this fruit; he
led with grace. He did not try to impress me with his knowledge or his
familiarity with "where I was coming from." He was genuine and gracious,
Christlike. His compassion and love opened the door for our relationship.

I'm sure I could construct practical strategies for building mentoring
relationships across cultures, but no strategy or tactic can work without
genuine compassion, humility and love from the mentor in the relationship. This is especially true if the mentor is from a race that has historically
held power. It is imperative that mentors of the majority culture enter
interracial mentor relationships with a servant's attitude and genuine love
and compassion.

---

6 Galatians 5:22-23 "But the fruit of the Spirit is love, joy, peace, patience, kindness, goodness, faithfulness,
  gentleness and self-control. Against such things there is no law."

No matter how many Bi-Semester services or Black Student Union panels Paul attended, he would never know what it was like to be a black man in America. He never pretended that he did. Sympathy for or knowledge about another culture, can never duplicate lived experience. Paul and I never would have been able to connect if he acted as if he knew all that there was to know about me just because he had some black friends or because he had read a few books. One mistake that mentors can make in an interracial relationship is to assume that they know anything about the other person before speaking to them. No one can be boiled down to a stereotype; we are all unique individuals, even in Christ. However, there are things about our cultures that shape us and mold us into the people that we've become. It is a beautiful dichotomy: our individual selves and the cultures that shape us. In an interracial mentoring relationship we must be willing to listen and to allow each individual to define him or herself.

My self is very different from Paul's self. We look nothing alike. I am a 6'4" dark skinned black man; Paul is a roughly 5'9" white man, with glasses. I'm bald headed and often mistaken for Malik Yoba of New York Undercover and Cool Runnings fame; Paul is more often mistaken for, well, I can't really think of anyone. Suffice it to say that he would never be mistaken for me. The music in our iPod's is different, though years of worshipping together may have led to some overlap. I would rather watch the Celtics than Paul's beloved Red Sox. Paul and I are different in just about every way. Nonetheless, we have an incredible relationship that will, I pray, last a lifetime.

I am excited about that! Paul never once felt the need to change who he was to be my mentor. In fact, it is because of who Paul is that he is able to be the amazing mentor that he is to me. Paul is the kind of man that I want to be. He is a great husband, a great father, a great leader, full of integrity; he doesn't need to change anything to be the kind of man that I would like to follow. The Apostle Paul says in 1 Corinthians 11:1 "Follow my example as I follow the example of Christ." I am trying to follow my good friend Paul, because it is clear that he is following in the footsteps of Christ. Furthermore, I would have lost respect for Paul if all of a sudden he started using slang and dressing differently when we interacted. It was important for me to see Paul as Paul if we were going to have any sort of real relationship.

As real and as great as our relationship is, there were some things that took a lot of getting used to with Paul. The strangest thing for me may have been the way that he was addressed by other members of the Fellowship on campus. When I was growing up, it was unheard of to call a preacher by his or her first name. In a traditional Black Baptist church calling your pastor by his or her first name is like calling your mother by her first name; that sort of thing is just not done.

It took me a while to get there with Paul.

Paul noticed my apprehension. He assured me that he was fine with both Reverend Sorrentino and Paul. He did not force me to move out of my comfort zone, but he did give me permission to do so. I was reluctant at first. I just would not call Reverend Sorrentino, "Paul." Then it dawned on me that it really was a cultural thing. This was something that I grew up with, a cultural understanding that felt natural to me but was foreign to everyone else. Eventually, I realized that this was not something worth holding onto. I should just call him Paul and see how it felt. One day I did it. From then on I was hooked! As I grew more comfortable with the concept of calling a member of the clergy by their first name, and as Paul and I became closer, in my heart he gradually became just "Paul". This little anecdote about names holds an important lesson for cross cultural relationships. A mentor must continuously give permission to those he is mentoring to step outside of their comfort zones, but he or she should never force them to do something that they are uncomfortable doing.

Looking back once again now on our first lunch together, over the distance of years, perhaps what strikes me most is the way Paul listened attentively to every word that I said during that meeting. His listening was not just attentive; he listened as a proud father would listen to his son. He listened as if every word I said was important. It is things as small as this, respecting me and actually listening to my words, which create unity. Even though neither one of us knew the other well, we were able to connect during that first lunch meeting.

This connection can't be described in words; it can't be written on paper. It is the best of Christian love, of Christian mentorship. And it was possible because Paul saw me as a Christian who was black, not as a Black Christian. In Paul's eyes, we were two people who had a shared culture in Christ rather than two people separated by differences in ethnic identity. Paul did not make the mistake that some people make of trying to be "color blind." Trying to ignore ethnic differences is unrealistic and potentially offensive as it seems to diminish a large portion of my identity.

God made me black for a reason, and that identity is too important to simply ignore! Paul was able to recognize that there were important differences between us, and to celebrate that difference. But at the deepest level he saw us as similar. And in this place of commonality, we were able to begin a beautiful friendship that will forever enrich each of our lives.

My interactions with Paul have had a transforming influence on the way that I interact with other brothers and sisters in Christ, particularly with older white men. God has allowed me to currently serve as the Pastor of a church which is about 90% white. Beyond this racial demographic, the majority of the congregation is older than me. In leadership meetings I am usually the youngest person in the room and the only black person in the room. If not for my experience and continued relationship with Paul, I would not be able to operate in my current environment. I am completely comfortable either mentoring or being mentored in these relationships, despite the age and ethnic differences. For that I credit my time spent with Paul. As I look back at our namesakes in the biblical text, I have only recently realized that the relationship between the Apostle Paul and his protégé Timothy in the Bible was cross cultural. Paul was Jewish; Timothy was of mixed Greek and Jewish heritage. God can do incredible work across cultures in mentoring relationships. Many Christians are missing out on life changing relationships because they are overlooking cross cultural mentoring opportunities.

Though he clapped off beat, and he stuck out like a sore thumb aesthetically, I have no doubt that God intended my good friend the Reverend Dr. Paul, to pray for me as I became a Reverend. I would not trade him for anyone in the world.

7

CHANGED TO BE A CHANGER

JONATHAN PEREZ WITH MATT MASCIOLI

When I arrived at Amherst College in the fall of 2003 I was not a Christian. On a good day I was an abstract deist, on a bad day an agnostic with strong atheist leanings. I considered myself a person of science. Anything more than a watchmaker God was impossible. As a child of privilege growing up in a reasonably affluent family in northern Virginia, physical want and deprivation were things I never experienced first-hand. I had never faced real physical hardship. Yet despite a wonderful and loving family, academic success, and admission to a great college—all the things the world tells us we should strive for—I arrived at Amherst with a deep emptiness inside of me, a yearning for something deeper than the superficiality of the world I saw all around me. I was lost and barely knew it.

I can now see that God was at work in my life in unexpected ways. It was not through my emptiness or loneliness that God brought me into contact with Himself and his Body, but through my commitment to community service, at a time when I had no desire to seek out God on my own. During January break, for reasons that I can only attribute to the hand of God, I agreed to sign-up for an Urban Plunge in Springfield, Massachusetts with the Amherst Christian Fellowship.

Springfield is the fourth largest city in New England with over 150,000 residents. Nearly a quarter live below the poverty line. The Urban Plunge was designed as a week of service in and among the community, joining with local Christian ministries and non-profits in their ongoing work. Looking at the schedule for the week, I noticed that each day had three major components: prayer in the morning, Bible study, and work projects in the afternoon. My dorm mate and friend Matt Mascioli, who had invited me on the trip, had told me that it was an explicitly Christian service week, but even he did not realize the extent to which Christ and His gospel would be front and center in all that we did. Despite my reservations, I agreed to go. God was at work.

During that Urban Plunge with the Nehemiah Community, an intentional Christian community in Springfield, I accepted Christ as my Lord and Savior. I have often wondered what it was that brought me to accept Christ that week. The simple answer is that He did. For the first time I encountered the Body of Christ, His people. In the Christian students on the trip and in the Nehemiah Community, I encountered the Gospel in its fullness. They were people who, although not perfect, were seeking to live out the Bible in their daily lives. Here were true Christians, not just Sunday worshipers. They sought to live each day according to their beliefs, both the easy and hard parts of what God's word has to say. Though they would freely admit that they were far from perfect, the Gospel was alive and moving in their lives. The reality of the Gospel was evident in their personal commitment to Jesus, as well as in their communal commitment to justice, racial reconciliation, and making Jesus known through their words and actions. I could not help but see its power shining through them. It was this, and not any overt message of repentance or salvation from sin, that attracted me to Christ. I saw the power of God at work in their lives and the joy and contentment of Christ in and amongst them, and I wanted to be a part of that.

On the third night of the trip, as I was interrogating Nehemiah Community member Patrick Murray about his faith, I came to the point where I decided to accept Christ. I do not remember the actual words of our conversation. I do know that at the end of the night we read the Apostles' Creed and prayed together the Lord's Prayer. I had little idea of what I was getting myself into with that simple decision to follow Christ that night, but after that turning point I knew I was committed.

After coming to Christ I knew that I needed to keep associating with people like those who brought me to Him, Christians who were actively living out their faith day to day. Upon returning to campus from the Urban Plunge in Springfield, I began attending the Amherst Christian Fellowship's meetings and events. I found a welcoming home. I did not really give it much conscious thought at the time, but in retrospect I think the reason I felt so at home in the Amherst Christian Fellowship was at least in part because of the multiethnic nature and diversity of the fellowship. Despite the differences in ethnicity and socioeconomic background, Amherst Christian Fellowship was a body of believers trying to live out their faith in Jesus Christ in the often challenging environment of Amherst College. The challenges presented by being together in fellowship across these lines gave the Fellowship an authenticity similar to that which I experienced in the Nehemiah Community in Springfield. In particular, I found a home amongst my fellow freshmen, many of whom had come on the Urban Plunge to Springfield and had been inspired by the challenge we had heard there to pursue social and economic justice. I joined the freshman prayer group. Together we formed a tight-knit community that was able to encourage and support each other in our respective walks with Christ. This group of freshmen also brought back to Amherst Christian Fellowship a strong passion for social and economic justice, ensuring that these values remained a core part of the fellowship.

From the beginning of my walk with Christ I saw racial reconciliation, multiethnicity, and social and economic justice as fundamental parts of what it truly means to live out the Gospel. These were the parts of Christianity that attracted me to it in the first place. However, it was during my time with Amherst Christian Fellowship that I learned to incorporate these concepts into my daily life.

Amherst Christian Fellowship's commitment to pursuing multiethnicity meant that when I first joined the fellowship I was joining a diverse body of believers. For me a multiethnic Body of Christ has always been the norm. Whereas most people grow up in a church that is ethnically and racially homogenous, I spent the foundational years of my walk with Christ in a fellowship that believed unity is integral to Christian discipleship. In working out this commitment to unity Amherst Christian Fellowship certainly experienced its fair share of challenges. But the pursuit of a multiethnic fellowship was something that we as a body were committed to. Going beyond just personal holiness, we strove to be one body across ethnic, social, and economic lines. We desired to bridge the gaps between rich and poor, share our resources, and draw together as a community of believers. As we struggled to live out these commitments, they were impressed deeply in my own heart and in the hearts of many of my fellow students. These ingrained values have continued to shape the life decisions that my peers and I have made since graduating from Amherst.

During my time at Amherst several other experiences further ingrained in me these core values. The first was my participation with several members of Amherst Christian Fellowship in the DeBerry Elementary School's Saturday school program in Springfield, Massachusetts. The program was started by the school's principal to help struggling students prepare for the state's standardized test, the Massachusetts Comprehensive Assessment System (MCAS). Our first contact with DeBerry Elementary had been through that first Urban Plunge. Several of us became regulars at the program over the next two years. Saturday mornings we drove to Springfield to tutor the students. After tutoring, we would go to the Nehemiah House for a Bible study, usually focused on what it means to embody the gospel, alongside its verbal proclamation. We explored the implications of what it means that all Christians, not just a select few, are called to pursue justice. We asked ourselves, "How can we proclaim the good news that the Kingdom of God has come, while at the same time ignoring the suffering of those around us?" Through those studies, I came to realize that the gospel is about an invitation to a radically different way of life in the here and now. To truly follow Christ means to be set apart not only by our words but by our very lives. My experiences working with these amazing children from a wide variety of ethnic backgrounds, though united by a common socio-economic background, deepened my concern for the marginalized.

A second significant experience was involvement with Amherst Homeless Connect, a group founded by Amherst Christian Fellowship students and almost entirely comprised of Christians from the campus. The group was formed by a number of freshman students following an Urban Plunge trip on which I had been a leader. A group of three pastors from Springfield churches had recently begun gathering several of their parishioners weekly to take food, blankets, and prayers to those living on the streets, with the hope of bringing both physical and spiritual help. Amherst Homeless Connect started with a small group of us gathering Monday nights and piling into a school van to drive to Springfield to meet the pastors and several of their parishioners. In those early days a dozen or so of us huddled in a circle on cold winter nights in the parking lot of the Basketball Hall of Fame. From those humble beginnings the ministry seemed to explode both on campus and off. During the 2007-2008 academic year we often needed a second van to fit all of the students. One night over 70 people gathered, including both students and Springfield church members. After three years the Monday group officially ended, in part because it had become too successful. So many folks were coming out that there was nothing for people to do. Furthermore, having thirty people all trying to help one person in the end actually undermines the purpose of the ministry, as those you are trying to reach end up seeming more like an exhibit than a person. But the outreach continues in small pockets as new individuals come forth in smaller numbers to continue the mission.

Late one winter evening in 2008, after we had been on the streets three hours and were preparing to head home, we saw two people hurriedly crossing the street carrying what looked like a garbage bag. Through experience, I had come to recognize most of the "regulars." I did not recognize these two. I had the driver of our van pull over; a few members of the group approached and made contact, and eventually called us over. The couple was indeed homeless and they were on their way to a nearby parking garage to spend the night. What struck me most about this couple was their youth, neat appearance, and the fact that they were married. We learned a bit about their story, what had brought them to the streets, and about how they had just recently been married but had no place to live. They were willing to go into the shelters for the night, but when we called we found that the woman's shelter was completely full. The husband was unwilling to leave his wife out on the street alone, and it seemed there was nothing we could do. Undeterred, pastors Greg Dyson of Springfield's Church in the Acres and Jim Munroe of Christ Church Cathedral decided that we weren't just going to leave this couple on the street that night. We drove them to the Marriot and rented them a room. Pastor Dyson and a group of students went with them up to the room where they had good conversation and powerful prayer.

It was during the Urban Plunge on which I was a leader that I felt God calling me to join the Nehemiah Community. I talked this over with members of the community, and over the next few months as I moved towards graduation as I applied to join and was invited in. Upon graduating from Amherst, I immediately moved into the Nehemiah Community in Springfield. My original plan was to spend maybe a year there before heading back to school to pursue a PhD in Biology. My hope was to spend the time learning how to function day to day in the midst of a secular world while still living out the central values of Christianity that had become so important to me. As I was preparing to move to Springfield, Nehemiah community members suggested that I consider joining AmeriCorps VISTA to work with the community's non-profit, Nehemiah Ministries, Inc., for a year. Ironically, the very idea of joining AmeriCorps was something that earlier in college I had dismissed as a waste of my time and talent. But God, through my time in Amherst Christian Fellowship, had changed me and given me a heart for ministry amongst the downtrodden and oppressed in urban centers. The call to live and do ministry in Springfield was not a radical change of life, but rather the next logical step on my journey.

Living and working amongst the marginalized populations of Springfield not only gave me a renewed heart for ministry in urban centers, but broke many of my remaining preconceptions and prejudices of the low-income and homeless. The people with whom I worked regularly ceased to be defined by their socioeconomic or racial status and became friends and colleagues. They ceased to be "them," and became friends, brothers and sisters. In the end, God's call for me to live in Springfield ended up spanning three years rather than the one year I had originally planned. They were three amazing years of spiritual growth, full of amazing friendships and ministry. During that time, I also discovered more about what it meant for my local church to embrace the values I had learned through the Amherst Christian Fellowship and the Nehemiah House. While in Springfield I joined Christ Church Cathedral and had the opportunity to witness and be involved with its various ministries amongst the poor and marginalized. During that time I also had the opportunity to work with Reverend Jim Munroe in leading our church to formally declare its commitment to justice by becoming a Just Peace Church.

A final lesson that I have learned from my time with Amherst Christian Fellowship and in the Nehemiah Community is that as a church we need to be living in community with one another as believers. The forms that this takes may vary greatly, but we as Christians need to risk venturing deeper into the shared common life that Christ calls us into. We must commit to sharing one another's joys and sorrows, triumphs and failures, and we must seek to become one body through all the struggles and challenges we face both individually and as a group. I learned that our witness for Christ is most powerful when we move beyond homogeneity to form communities that cross social, economic, and ethnic divides, when we truly embrace one another in words and deeds as brothers and sisters in Christ.

Amherst Christian Fellowship provided the framework and support for me to grow as a Christian during those first years, and ingrained in me a commitment to strive for racial reconciliation and justice in the church and world. It is in the body of Christ that I have found my eternal home. I may not fit a particular mold of Christian perfectly, but that is the beauty of the Kingdom of God—none of us quite fits in. It is only by the grace of God that we are able to come to God as one body, across all dividing lines, to live as servants and witnesses of Christ. The values I learned in my earliest days as a Christian have stayed with me beyond Amherst, and I pray that the churches and cities in which I live will be greatly impacted as a result of my attempt to live out those values.

PART 2
THEORY & PRACTICE

We hope that our story in Part one helped you to think along with us and process some of the same concerns that moved each of us. In this second section we more systematically take on both the theoretical and practical questions that arise from a commitment to multiethnic fellowship.

We begin with the sociological and socioeconomic realities of our world, examining the complexities of race in America. Following this foundational chapter, which confront us with the realities of race in America and in the church, we turn to practical questions. How can we foster genuine multiethnic relationships? How should leadership function in a multiethnic fellowship? How will a multiethnic fellowships need to be structured differently in order to succeed? What about multiethnic worship? Finally, how can we confront the power of racism in the church?

We hope that our efforts to explore these questions will inspire you on your journey toward racial reconciliation, give you sound biblical and ethical reasons for pursuing multiethnic fellowship and equip you with practical skills for multiethnic ministry.

8

THE REALITIES OF RACIAL INEQUALITY

PAUL SORRENTINO

One day one of the student leaders of the Fellowship came by my office. Liza was committed to the direction we were heading in becoming an intentional, multiethnic fellowship. The leaders had decided together to spend more time together outside of formal activities to deepen their relationships. The other leaders occasionally wanted to skip the pre-paid meals in the dining hall and go into town for a meal or they wanted to go into town late at night for pizza or ice cream. This seemed like a great idea. However, it created problems for the student in my office. Liza wanted to be with the other student leaders, but she could not afford to go and did not want to underscore her situation by asking someone else for help.

Liza was on a full scholarship and she worked in the library for spending money. By being very careful with her budgeting, she had just enough money to cover her expenses and do her laundry. She had no discretionary money. Such a dilemma had simply not occurred to me. The other leaders had come up with a good approach to relationship building, but no one, except the student in my office, needed to think about the relatively small financial expenditure involved. While we had been thinking about our need to be racially and ethnically inclusive, we had made our focus too narrow. We could not just add "ethnic inclusivity" to our list of projects like "have a small group for seniors." When we think about overcoming a racial divide, we are talking about much more than just skin color and ethnic heritage. Along with those two things come a host of other factors that are influential in building genuine relationships across difference. As Christians, we need to be concerned about the whole person: such things as family, education, income, housing, employment as well as spiritual growth. Majority people often have the freedom to ignore some concerns, such as the cost of a pizza, because their life circumstances free them to focus on the particular situation at hand. This is not to say that white people do not face difficulties. Rather, it is to say that, on average, minorities face disadvantages on a variety of variables that together define the racial divide in the United States. This racial divide is real, it is measurable, and its reality is firmly established in social science research. Again, this is not to say that only people of color struggle with issues of injustice and economic hardship. Nor is race or ethnicity the only way people are defined. We have multiple influences and points of identification. We think about ourselves, and others, in any number of ways: violinist, football player, attractive, computer geek, Spanish speaking, Methodist, intelligent, electrician, funny, single, woman, or second generation immigrant. Race is one key way that people are identified and grouped in our society, but it is more than just that. Race correlates with serious and significant sociological and socioeconomic differences that have a profound impact on people's lives. Christians have an obligation to be aware of these differences and to consider them if we are to be good neighbors.

During the presidential campaign of 2008, then Senator Barack Obama, in a speech at Constitution Center in Philadelphia entitled "A More Perfect Union," made such a call to take issues of race seriously:

> ...race is an issue that I believe this nation cannot afford to ignore right now...the comments that have been made and the issues that have surfaced over the last few weeks reflect the complexities of race in this country that we've never really worked through—a part of our union that we have yet to perfect. And if we walk away now, if we simply retreat into our respective corners, we will never be able to come together and solve challenges like health care, or education, or the need to find good jobs for every American (Obama March 18, 2008).

In his speech, Obama made several crucial points about issues of race. First, race issues are complex and hard to address. They are complex because of multiple layers of history, heritage, suffering, interdependent responsibility and other factors. Second, this is a conversation that we should not and must not avoid. Third, the complex issue of race is not a factor in isolation, but it relates to most every aspect of our society. Race affects how we go about addressing entrenched problems that are a concern to all of us. We cannot solve many of society's problems without taking race into account.

Christians have a special call by God to care for those who suffer injustice and oppression. White evangelicals were largely uninvolved with the civil rights movement during the 1960s. Today the church, especially the evangelical church, has an opportunity to address the silent and spoken pleas of those who suffer within our society.

Research shows that there is a significant and clear disparity between racial groups in the United States. We begin by looking at the realities of race in the Church.

RACE IN THE CHURCH

According to Michael Emerson of Rice University, United States congregations are not just highly segregated but hypersegregated. Places of worship are more segregated than schools, businesses and neighborhoods. Neighborhoods were found to be three to ten times more racially diverse than the congregations located within them. There are between 300,000 and 350,000 places of worship in the United States. Of these, 92.5 percent are what Emerson calls "racially homogeneous," with 80 percent or more of the congregation from one race. Christian congregations number approximately 270,000. Of these, eighty-four percent are Protestant and seven percent Catholic. Five percent of Protestant congregations and fifteen percent of Catholic congregations are racially mixed. Protestant churches can be further divided into conservative (62 percent) and mainline (38 percent). Six percent of conservative Protestant congregations were racially mixed and three percent of mainline Protestant churches (Emerson and Woo 2006, 34-46). Emerson defines a multiracial congregation as one with 80 percent or less of one race. This number provides a "critical mass" of other races so that people of the dominant race have a high probability of interacting with people of other races (DeYoung, Emerson et al. 2003, 76).

Evangelical churches that are dominantly white face special challenges in reaching across the racial divide. Evangelicals, on average, spend more time involved with their own church group activities than Christians from other traditions. This leaves little time for people outside of their own church, which is already, largely, racially segregated. The programming commitments of many evangelical churches serve to limit opportunities for significant contacts with people who are not already a part of their congregation.

Emerson and Smith found that the historical patterns, theology and the congregational practices of evangelical Christians substantially hindered them from having a positive effect in reducing racism (Emerson 2000, 133). Evangelicals tend to be highly relational and individualistic in their theology. They tend to focus on individual responsibility and individual relationships, with God and with each other. Thus evangelicals may establish friendships with people of different races and ethnicities. They may ask forgiveness for individual offenses. They may do their best not to discriminate. But such an emphasis on individual relationships does little to encourage evangelicals to address the structural inequities described in the rest of this chapter.

Another barrier which may prevent the church from effectively addressing issues of race is what Lee Nash refers to as the "miracle motif." According to this way of thinking, Christian maturity is a result of conversion and all other problems are treated as solved or unimportant once a person is converted. The miracle motif, according to Emerson and Smith, "directs the church to become so focused on evangelizing that new converts are taught that Christian maturity consists of preparing for and actually evangelizing, to the exclusion of taking on social responsibility" (Ibid., 131). Once a person is "right with God" everything else will fall into place. In one sense, this lets evangelicals off the hook. Responsibility for improving conditions depends on an individual's faith in God and his or her own behavior. God changes lives and the rest follows. This is not to say that evangelicals do not help others. Church members do an enormous amount to assist people need. However, despite a great deal of time, money and energy spent to help individuals, congregations may do little to address negative societal or structural issues. These are largely ignored (Ibid., 130-31).

Emerson and Smith conclude with a pointed indictment of evangelical approaches to social issues:

> ...the white evangelical prescriptions do not address major issues of racialization. They do not solve such structural issues as inequality in health care, economic inequality, police mistreatment, unequal access to educational opportunities, racially imbalanced environmental degradation, unequal political power, residential segregation, job discrimination, or even congregational segregation. White evangelical solutions do not challenge or change the U.S. society that "allocates differential economic, political, social, and even psychological rewards" to racial groups (Emerson 2000, 132).

There is a tall library at the University of Massachusetts, Amherst. It is a lovely building, but after it was completed two major design flaws came to light. First, bricks would fall off regularly. Second, the design engineer forgot to include the weight of the books in his calculations. This means that only every other floor can be used to shelve books. The problem of falling bricks has been resolved, but the structural problem for weight bearing books has not. White evangelicals have often done the hard work of replacing bricks, but less often considered deeper structural issues. In what follows, I present some of these structural inequalities.

Data released by the Census Bureau for 2005, summarized in Table 1, shows a disparity in education and income according to race.

	Asian American	White	Hispanic	Black
Have College Degree	49%	30%	17%	12%
Median Income	$60,367	$50,622	$36,278	$30,939

Table 1: Education and income data from 2005 Census (Source: Factfinder 2005)

The income of blacks was 61 percent that of whites while Hispanics earned 72 percent as much as whites. Income level for black households has remained at about the same proportion to that of white households since 1980. While Asian Americans enjoy high income levels, the poverty rate for Asian Americans is higher and home ownership rates lower than those of whites. The high number of college degrees among Asian Americans indicates a wide gap between those at the top and those at the bottom.

Home ownership for whites increased dramatically after World War II due to government programs and credit availability. These programs were largely unavailable for blacks and other minorities because of discriminatory practices. Even when the inequitable practices are no longer in place, home ownership disparities continue because the legacy of home ownership is passed on to whites in much larger proportion than to minorities (Ohlemacher). As a result, the average white baby boomer stands to inherit $65,000 while his or her black baby boomer counterpart will inherit $8,000 (Jackson 2000).

Melvin Oliver (University of California, Santa Barbara) and Thomas Shapiro (Brandeis University) conducted a landmark study comparing economic standing by race. They present their findings in *Black Wealth/ White Wealth: A New Perspective on Racial Inequality.* They say that "wealth" is a better basis for economic comparison than "income" alone (Emerson 2000, 13).

Oliver and Shapiro used two principle measures of financial well-being. The first was net worth. Net worth is all of one's assets minus all of one's debts. The second measure, net financial assets, may be a more important indicator of wealth and financial stability. Net financial assets, is determined by taking net worth and subtracting any equity accrued on a home, vehicle or other property. When the net worth and net financial assets of blacks and whites are compared (Table 2) the disparities are staggering (Emerson 2000, 13-14)

	Median net worth (assets – debts)		Median net financial assets (net worth – equity)	
	White	Black	White	Black
Overall	43,800	3,700	7,000	0
Upper white-collar occupation (UWC)	66,800	12,303	15,150	5
UWC & UWC parents	70,850	17,499	16,420	5
College graduates	74,922	17,437	19,823	175

Table 2: White and black household median net worth and net financial assets by selected characteristics in dollars (Source: Emerson 2000, 14)

In addition to an overall comparison, Table 2 further breaks down the results into three categories: Those working in upper white-collar jobs (UWC); those from this first category whose parents also had upper white-collar positions (UWC & UWC Parents); and college graduates. White-collar jobs refer to employment that is salaried and not manual labor. Upper white-collar jobs include above average salaries.

Median net financial assets is an indicator of what is likely to happen if a person's equity is taken away. When equity is not considered, the overall difference between whites and blacks is $7,000 to $0. In other words, blacks rely almost solely on income while whites have reserve assets as a cushion. When the economy is weak, such as during the sub-prime mortgage crisis of 2008, people without a financial cushion and whose job situation is uncertain are in the greatest danger of losing assets and are therefore the most vulnerable.

EMPLOYMENT

Whites tend to have more prestigious and better paying jobs. Blacks are more likely to be in low-prestige, lower paying jobs. Blacks are twice as likely as whites to be unemployed. This ratio has held constant since 1950 (Emerson 2000, 12).

An MIT study conducted in 2002 demonstrates bias in hiring according to perception of race by name alone. A "too black" name like Tamika Jackson was 50 percent less likely to gain an interview for a job than her equally qualified white counterpart named Anne Murphy (Jung 2007).

Employment discrimination charges filed with the U.S. Equal Employment Opportunity Commission (EEOC) have been rising in the last five years. The single highest category of discrimination filed in 2007 was for racial discrimination. Of all charges filed, 37 percent were race-related, the highest percentage since 1994. Racial discrimination filings rose 12 percent from 2006 to 2007. To put these numbers in context, the second highest category of discrimination filings after "race" was "retaliation" at 32 percent of all charges filed; religious discrimination charges were seventh at 4 percent. This was a new record for religious discrimination filings, increasing 13 percent from 2006 and doubling the number of filings in 1992. Comparison with other categories of filings indicates how significant and long standing are the number of race-related discrimination filings (Millman 2007).

HEALTH

African American and Latino children are twelve times more likely than white children to live in "double jeopardy." "Double jeopardy" means that a person is in a low-income family and a poor neighborhood. An average poor white child lives in a neighborhood with a 13.6 percent poverty rate. The typical poor African American or Latino child has a neighborhood poverty rate of 30 and 26 percent respectively. The study, "Toward a Policy-Relevant Analysis of Geographic and Racial/Ethnic Disparities in Child Health," found that one's neighborhood is a significant factor in health disparities based on race and ethnicity. The authors concluded that "Segregated, disadvantaged neighborhoods limit economic advancement for minorities due to limited job and educational opportunities, as well as poor return on housing investment; expose minorities to violent crime, environmental hazards, poor municipal services, and a lack of healthy food options; and lead to segregated and poorer quality healthcare settings" (Digest 2008).

These factors are reflected in the shorter life expectancy for African Americans compared to whites. African Americans, both male and female, are about 10 percent more likely than their white counterparts to have high blood pressure (hypertension). In 2003, the age adjusted mortality rate from hypertension for African American males was 49.7 per 1000,000 while it was 14.9 percent for white males. The comparable rate for women was 40.8 per 100,000 for blacks and 14.5 per 100,000 for whites. Between 2000 and 2004, the infant mortality rate (IMR) for African American babies was 13.5 per 1,000 live births. For American Indian babies the IMR rate was 8.7 per 1,000. This compares with the white infant IMR of 5.7 per 1,000 live births (University of Wisconsin School of Medicine 2008).

EDUCATION

Disparate opportunities in education also begin early. Preschool has been demonstrated to be a significant advantage in education. It is largely whites who are able to pay the cost for enrollment in private preschools. Head Start programs serve less than one-half of low income children qualifying for programming. A full 60 percent of these are children of color (Jung 2007).

According to a 2004 report by The Civil Rights Project at Harvard University, white high school students in the United States have a 74.9 percent graduation rate. Asian/Pacific Islander students graduated at the highest rate of 76.8 percent. These compared with graduation rates for Hispanic students at 53.2 percent, American Indian students at 51.1 percent and black high school students graduating at a rate of 51.1 percent. Nearly one-half of all black, Hispanic and American Indian students who enter high school do not graduate (American Bar Association, Presidential Advisory Council on Diversity in the Profession, October 2005, 2).

According to the U.S. Department of Education standardized testing, at the age of 17, blacks and Hispanics score at about the same level in reading and math as white 13-year-olds (Perie and Moran 2005).

ENTERTAINMENT

There are significant parallels between the ways people think about television entertainment and how they evaluate experience in church. As a result, television viewing preferences can be helpful in thinking about perceptions of race in the church.

Through the 1990s blacks and whites television preferences differed significantly. In 1995-6 viewing season, only two television shows, NFL Monday Night Football and ER, were in the top 20 for both blacks and whites. And although ER was the number one show among whites, it was 20th among blacks. Seinfeld, number two for whites, was only 89th for blacks (Emerson 2000, 16).

Since the 1990s television viewing habits have changed dramatically. By 2007, 10 programs were in the top 20 both for African Americans and the total U.S. population. Likewise, Asian American viewers had 11 programs in common with the broader population's top 20. This change may be explained in part by the networks' increasing commitment to cast people of color in starring roles. Many of today's television shows now have casts that resemble the diversity of our society. A broader audience can identify with the characters so the viewership has increased (Young 2007).

INCARCERATION

Of every 100 people in the United States, one is in prison. Among Latino men this ratio rises to one of every 36. One of every 15 black men is imprisoned. The ratio increases to one out of nine for black men between 20 and 34 years of age. The rate for white men in the same age range is below one percent (one out of 106). Among women ages 35-39, one of every 355 white women is incarcerated while one of 100 black women is imprisoned (Hannah 2007).

Unfair sentencing guidelines contribute to the large numbers of blacks incarcerated. Crack cocaine and powder cocaine have similar affects on users and are different forms of the same drug. Penalty for the use or distribution of these drugs, however, differs at a 1 to 100 ratio. For crack cocaine, the less expensive drug generally found in poorer communities, a mandatory penalty of five years is triggered by distribution or possession of five grams. For powder cocaine, the more expensive drug, a mandatory five year sentence does not kick in until the amount reaches 500 grams (Alliance 2008).

RACISM

Racism in the United States may seldom appear overt and obvious, particularly to whites. Jim Crow laws no longer exist. The Ku Klux Klan is far less evident than it once was. Today's racism is likely to be in the form of what social scientists call "aversive racism." Aversive racism "represents a subtle, often unintentional form of bias that characterizes many White Americans who possess strong egalitarian values and who believe that they are nonprejudiced" (Dovidio, Gaertner et al. 2002, 90). The word "aversive" reflects two components of this racism. First, aversive racism is characterized by an underlying anxious reaction to people of color. The person may be unaware of this reaction. It is likely to lead to avoidance and social awkwardness in interactions, but not open hostility. A second component of aversive racism is a strong belief in racial egalitarianism that makes any hint that he or she may be prejudiced aversive to him or herself (Dovidio, Gaertner et al. 2002, 91). Research has shown that evaluating racial bias is further complicated because whites tend to focus on their external interactions and outward behavior while blacks pay attention to underlying attitudes and motives, reflecting a classic difference between verbal and non-verbal communication (Dovidio, Gaertner et al. 2002, 98).

Aversive racism shows itself in subtle comments. For example, "You are so articulate" can be taken to mean, I would not expect someone of your race to be so intelligent. "There is only one race, the human race" may come across to a person of color as a denial of their culture and heritage. "I believe the most qualified person should get the job" may imply that people of color get jobs because of race and not competence (Sue, Capo-dilupo et al. 2007, 276).

These examples give an idea of the complexity of inter-racial commu-nication. Whites will often focus on external statements, while people of color often look for underlying meaning. The deep-seated nature of preju-dice, which I believe we all carry, makes it crucial for us to meaningfully interact with people different than ourselves. It is in doing so that we are most likely to become aware of the prejudice that we may harbor and examine that prejudice in the light of God's love for all people and to ask for God's help in correcting our attitude. We need to work to make our conscious and unconscious attitudes congruent.

A common definition of racism is "prejudice plus power." Beverly Tatum, president of Spelman College, rejects that definition because she finds that many of her students think of themselves as neither prejudiced nor power-ful. Instead, she prefers David Wellman's definition of racism as "a system of advantage based on race" (Tatum 1997, 7). By this definition racism is more than personal attitudes and prejudice, and involves systemic power. "A system of advantage" includes policies and practices on an institutional and societal level, including access to better schools, housing, and employ-ment. These systemic advantages work in concert to benefit one segment of society at the detriment of another (Tatum 1997, 7-8).

Tatum differentiates between two types of racism. She defines active racism as "blatant, intentional acts of racial bigotry and discrimination." (Tatum 1997, 11) By contrast, passive racism takes more subtle forms that might include laughing at racist jokes or not challenging racist practices in the work place.

To illustrate the difference, Tatum uses an analogy of people walking on a moving airport walkway. Active racists walk rapidly on the moving con-veyor belt. Active racists are readily apparent as they zoom by those simply standing. Passive racists, however, stand on the moving conveyor belt and are simply carried along. Passive racists do not have to do anything but they will still get to the same place as the fast moving active racists.

The person symbolically standing on the conveyor belt may not be conscious of the benefits she is receiving, but it is a benefit that accrues to her nonetheless. The only way to avoid being moved in the same direction as the active racist is to turn and go the other way. Such action will require deliberate and intentional movement in order to overcome the ongoing, opposite movement of the conveyor belt (Tatum 1997, 11-12).

This is the systemic racism that we encounter in the United States and that is documented in the statistics above. People within the system of racial inequality who simply continue to live as they have always lived face unintended consequences. Unless actively challenged, a racialized system works for the benefit of the majority, whites, those standing or walking on the conveyor belt, and to the disadvantage of people of color. The church's mandate to "do justly" (Micah 6:8) requires us be system interrupters for the sake of the gospel.

9

WHERE EVERYONE IS UNCOMFORTABLE
AND THAT'S OKAY

PAUL SORRENTINO

Crossing racial and ethnic divides is not easy, but it is worth it. One spring, our fellowship took some time to talk about how things were going for us as a multiethnic fellowship. We had spent time in racial specific groupings (Asian, black, Latino, mixed, and white), then we came together as a whole group to share our thoughts. When each group had finished talking, I said: "This is great. ACF can have a new motto: 'Where everyone is uncomfortable.'" One of our black students quickly added, emphatically, "And that's okay!" This is the reality of a multiethnic fellowship. Everyone needs to be a little uncomfortable in order to serve the needs of the wider body. That is what it means to be a servant of Christ.

SHARING RESPONSIBILITY

A fellowship is not multiethnic unless responsibility and authority is shared. It is not enough to have a smattering of people of different ethnicities in attendance. People of different races and cultures need to be in positions of decision-making and visible leadership. This is not tokenism, but a way of being certain that God's voice is heard through the various heritages, ethnicities, and experiences of those God has brought into the community. We all have "blind spots" that cause us to distort what might be clear to others. We therefore need one another in order to "see."

Having people of different ethnicities and races in visible leadership roles is another way of helping people to feel welcome. Just as with television viewing preferences, when people see others who look like themselves in leadership roles, it makes a significant difference in the way they feel. When people ethnically similar to me fill visible and substantial roles, it communicates an assurance that I too will be valued and have a voice in what happens in this group. When only majority leadership is evident, then the opposite message about minority involvement is communicated.

This principle of shared responsibility was demonstrated through the first internal crisis in the early church. In Acts 6:1-7 Luke reports that Greek speaking Jews felt discriminated against because their widows were passed over in the church's food distribution:

> *In those days when the number of disciples was increasing, the Hellenistic Jews among them complained against the Hebraic Jews because their widows were being overlooked in the daily distribution of food.* (Acts 6:1)

The problem faced by the Church was one of difference and disparity between a minority and a majority in the community. The Hellenistic Jewish widows, those not raised in Jerusalem who had adopted Greek language and culture, were not receiving the daily food distribution. They were "outsiders" and did not receive the same treatment as the Hebraic Jewish widows who were born in Israel and spoke Aramaic. Hence, the Hellenistic Jews complained to the leaders. Taking care of widows and the needy was an important Jewish value that the newly developing church took seriously (Deut. 15:11; 25:19-22; Ps. 68:5). Some people might call this overlooking of the Hellenistic widows "benign neglect." Others might say that the Hellenists should have stayed where they belonged. But the Apostles took the problem seriously.

The Apostles' solution to the problem is usually taken as a lesson about leadership and the appointment of deacons in the church:

> *So the Twelve gathered all the disciples together and said, "It would not be right for us to neglect the ministry of the word of God in order to wait on tables. Brothers and sisters, choose seven men from among you who are known to be*

full of the Spirit and wisdom. We will turn this responsibility over to them and
will give our attention to prayer and the ministry of the word."

This proposal pleased the whole group. They chose Stephen, a man full of
faith and of the Holy Spirit; also Philip, Procorus, Nicanor, Timon, Parmenas,
and Nicolas from Antioch, a convert to Judaism. They presented them to the
apostles, who prayed and laid their hands on them. (Acts 2:2-6)

While this passage is about leadership and does establish a pattern for
the appointment of deacons, the truly revolutionary thing that happened
in the Jerusalem church in Acts 6 was recognition of the need to take account of minorities.

The apostles disregarded the cultural prejudices of the day and did
something radical. In the language of Perkins and Rice from *More Than
Equals*, the leadership admitted there was a problem, they submitted to the
Hellenistic minority, and they committed to a plan of action to right the
systemic injustice (Perkins and Rice 1993). The apostles chose to elevate
the minority group to a place of significant and shared leadership by ap-
pointing seven Greek speaking believers, "full of the Spirit and wisdom," to
take responsibility for the food distribution. This must have been a startling
response for the Jerusalem-bred believers who were simply maintaining
the status quo by keeping "better qualified" believers in leadership.

After this groundbreaking innovation the church demonstrated a Jesus-
type love for one another that threatened to overturn the cultural status-
quo. Luke reports the results:

So the word of God spread. The number of disciples in Jerusalem increased
rapidly, and a large number of priests became obedient to the faith. (Acts 6:7)

While there may not be a definitive cause-effect relationship, it seems
that this leadership change was a significant precursor to both rapid growth
and increased persecution in the Church.

The Acts 6 incident can be understood through a grid that Carl Ellis
refers to as a "window of marginalization." (Figure 1) The grid evaluates

marginalization on four variables., with four resulting quadrants. Relational marginalization takes place in direct, personal interactions. Systemic marginalization happens because of traditional social conventions. Marginalization by design is intentional. Marginalization by default is unintended and comes about due to a genuine or perceived lack of power.

	Marginalization by design	Marginalization by default
Relational marginalization	X	
Systemic marginalization		

Figure 1: Carl Ellis's "Window of Marginalization" (Ellis, December 12, 2001)

An example of relational marginalization by design took place when a black student I know of from another campus attended his first class. After class, the professor told him, "you better drop this class because, if you don't, you're going to flunk it, and if you ever say anything to anyone it'll be your word against mine." Relational marginalization by default coincides with "aversive racism," discussed in chapter 8, where statements may not be intended as hurtful, but reflect an underlying bias that is nevertheless harmful. For example, a Latino church member makes an announcement and, afterward, another church member compliments the person on how articulate she is. The underlying message seems to communicate surprise that this Latino could be articulate. Ellis offers a case of systemic marginalization by design when he recounts how an elderly black man was required to address all whites, including a young boy, as "Mister so and so." Systemic marginalization by default occurs when circumstances are weighted against someone, even when intentions are good. For example, a student who attended an underperforming school may be accepted at an outstanding college. However, if there are no remedial support services provided to make up for his poor quality education, he is likely to perform poorly compared to a student educated at an elite preparatory school. (Ellis 2001).

In Acts 6 systemic marginalization of Hellenistic Jews was likely by default rather than by design. The believers from Jerusalem probably did not think about it much. Naturally, they thought, one must pay special attention to those we know — to "our own kind." The Twelve, also from Judea, might have chosen to make excuses for themselves and the other Judean believers since their behavior was unintentional. Significantly, they did not.

Individuals, who are part of a majority, if they address marginalization at all, tend to focus on the relational marginalization by design quadrant (the X above). The work of Perkins and Rice, which has been so influential in the shaping of the Amherst Christian Fellowship, has focused on this area of racial reconciliation. Addressing relational marginalization by design is the most natural starting point for dialogue across racial lines, and it is an important one.

If the dialogue does not move beyond the upper left quadrant, however, then some of the most significant needs of minorities will not be addressed. Further, even if relational issues are being attended to within the context of the fellowship, there is a strong likelihood that people of color will be marginalized by a failure to examine their needs related to the other three quadrants. The expectations and values of "committed" majority fellowship members may themselves militate against considering the other quadrants (Emerson 2000).

The window of marginalization grid is an ever-present tension for people of color. We hope and pray that the fellowship can be a place that is largely free of racism by design and default. Even if it is, however, people of color live much of their lives "waiting for the other shoe to drop" in their interactions with majority culture people. This means that, until relationships and trust are well developed, there is always a degree of wariness which seems tiresome for the person of color. Initially, when people of color are asked to be committed to a predominantly majority fellowship, they are being asked a great deal. Stylistically there may be dramatic differences in the way people pray, sing and preach. These take getting used to and mean giving up what is natural and comfortable for them.

People of their own ethnic communities may belittle them and call them derogatory names such as "oreo," "coconut" or "banana." The very existence of these terms points to the racial divide between those who are white and those who are not. There may be a perception that a person of color is abandoning his or her own racial and ethnic identity in order to appear white. In addition to animosity from people within one's own ethnic group, minority individuals may feel isolation in majority communities because members of the majority are surrounded by what they know and people with whom they identify. As an African American friend said to me:

> There isn't necessarily any need (for whites) to reach out to students of color in a community setting because their comfort is retained with very little effort. This therefore leads to the student of color having to take on the task of assimilating for the sake of preserving the comfort of members of the majority and partaking in community fellowship at all, with members of the majority tending towards comments like, "oh, you are just like us." I was told this once, actually. I was at Christian school, and the teacher brought up something about race, and one student turned to me and said, "Don't worry, _____. You aren't really black to us." Because to them, I reflected everything familiar to them about themselves, their culture and their church views. My skin just happened to be the wrong color. They weren't aware of how much I had to leave at the door every time I went to school.

In a multiethnic setting, there is no shared ethnic or cultural heritage. Jokes are understood differently, or not understood at all. A person of color therefore faces significant obstacles in joining a Christian fellowship that is not of his/her own ethnicity. Most of us want church to be a place where we feel "at home" and comfortable. We want to focus on God and not worry about other distractions. People of color are far more likely to feel "at home" in the comfort of their own ethnic culture and background, just as whites do. I underscore this because I want majority people to know that people of color give up something when they join a majority white church. True, they will gain some things, but the costs should not be underestimated.

People of color may well benefit from avenues of support outside of the fellowship. Such external involvements are a way that leaders can champion people of color who are involved in a multiethnic fellowship. These outside commitments, however, also make it difficult for them to be as actively involved in the fellowship as a majority person who does not have these additional responsibilities and relationship needs

A person of color may be an effective small group bible study leader within his or her own ethnic context, but be unprepared to lead in the typical inductive method used by most majority campus groups and churches. He or she may be used to a style of leadership that is more didactic. This is an opportunity to learn from the strengths of each approach. Sometimes a small group geared toward a particular ethnic group will better serve its members by utilizing the teaching style members are most used to in their own tradition. In Amherst Christian Fellowship, we encourage ethnic-specific small groups. They do not need to be limited exclusively to a specific ethnic group, but should only include people of other ethnicities who have a commitment to this group and a willingness to sit under a style of leadership to which they may be unaccustomed. These ethnic-specific groups also meet some of the needs mentioned in the paragraph immediately above.

In Amherst Christian Fellowship, our goal is to have representatives from all ethnicities involved in the fellowship at every level of leadership. As mentioned above, this helps us to "hear" and "see" better. We have also tried to involve as many students as possible in leadership. We have numerous leadership teams, including executive board, music team, small group leaders, Friday night fellowship team, prayer team, communications & publicity, social council, and outreach. We are quite decentralized. Our leadership groups are like squads of a football team — not separate teams competing against each other, but segments of the same team. Just as defensive backs, defensive line, offensive line, receivers, punters and kickers, and quarterbacks meet separately to prepare for a game, so our teams meet separately to prepare for their roles. We do have regular "game day" celebrations where everyone connected with the Fellowship can be involved and present at the same time. Churches have natural opportunities for "game days" on Sundays.

When I refer to "sharing responsibility," I do not mean a diminishment of whites, but an elevation of people of color so that we have parity. All of us are to use our personalities, backgrounds, and gifts for the sake of the kingdom. I appreciated what black minister Alex Gee had to say at Urbana 2000. Following Brenda Salter-McNeil's talk on racial reconciliation Gee affirmed majority people and said, "We need you to be white!" He then encouraged us to use our power for godly ends.

COMMUNITY, PRIORITIES & CHALLENGES

We have found Willow Creek Community Church's definition of community useful. We want Amherst Christian Fellowship to be a place where we can know and be known, serve and be served, love and be loved, and celebrate and be celebrated. To these we have added a fifth characteristic. Our community must be a place where we can forgive and be forgiven. It is inevitable that we will step on one another's toes and offend each other in ways we cannot foresee as well as ways of which we are aware. Living out the gospel in a committed multiethnic community always means that we seek grace and forgiveness from one another. When we do that, we have the privilege of experiencing the transforming grace of God. We are changed by our life in Christian community. As John wrote, "But if we walk in the light, as he is in the light, we have fellowship with one another, and the blood of Jesus, his Son, purifies us from all sin." (1 John 1:7)

Interacting with people of different ethnicities and cultures is a wonderful way to develop our Christian character. When we are comfortable in our own environment, it is easy to convince ourselves that we are much better than we are. When we are around other people, especially those far different from ourselves, we cannot help but run smack into our own prejudices, fears, and misconceptions. Then we can choose to do something about them. Fellowship is a wonderful means of purification from sin.

In Amherst Christian Fellowship, we encourage people to have outside activities. This serves to strengthen our mission of being "salt and light" in the world and, at Amherst, it helps us fulfill the College's motto, *Terras Irradient* ("Let them illuminate the earth"). This diffuse involvement does create a challenge in developing community, but if people have a sense that they are welcomed and loved, there will be community. A Christian organization that is constantly drawing its people into meaningful fellowship and sending them back out into the world is a healthy community, or at least heading in the right direction. Despite the richness of community interaction, unity in Christ should not be an end in itself, but should contribute to advancing the kingdom of God.

In a multiethnic community, trust is a leader's most valuable asset. Trust is difficult to gain and easy to lose. If people believe that you are not trying to manipulate them or use them, then good relationships can develop, as can trust. To establish trust I have found it vital that I be clear in what I am saying, mean what I say, and keep my word. I need to develop a genuine appreciation for the things that matter to others. When people know that they are more important to me than my own agenda, they will grow to trust me. Valuing what is important to others also means changing some of my priorities so that I can be present with them to enjoy and appreciate the things they value.

We build community as we listen to people's hearts' desires and together seek God's wisdom. Several years ago, a majority student believed God wanted him to be an editor for the school newspaper. He was a student leader in the Fellowship who helped lead our Friday Night Fellowship meetings and led a small group. He would have to give up these key roles if he were to take on a greater responsibility with the newspaper. Despite my reluctance to see it happen, as we talked and prayed it seemed like a wise decision. It was consistent with his field of study and long-term goals, and he clearly saw it as an avenue for ministry. His small group supported him by praying regularly for him and asking him how things were going. This student has now completed his PhD in English and is following Christ as a college professor.

A Latina pre-med student had been an outstanding small group leader during her sophomore year. Her dream was to become a physician and to return to serve her community in southern California. She told me that her junior year would be incredibly demanding academically and that she would need to "disappear" for the year. As we talked this through, it was evident that she was struggling with the desire to be both a responsible student and a faithful follower of Christ. We decided, for the sake of her spiritual and emotional health, that she would come only to our Friday Night Fellowship and that, otherwise, she would focus on her studies. She had a network of friends who would pray for her and support her. She also committed to coming to a week-long camp at the end of the year and leading a small group in her senior year. She did both of those things. She has now graduated from medical school and is working at a southern California clinic with her husband, whom she met in medical school.

When my family and I came back from a year's study leave in Vancouver, the fellowship was in a rebuilding phase. A key leader was a Taiwanese American student. She sensed God calling her to study abroad in Taiwan, where her father and some of her family still lived. The fellowship was just gaining momentum, and it was hard to even think of her leaving at that point. Yet, her presence in Taiwan proved to be important for her and her family. Her father, who lived in Taiwan, unexpectedly died while she was there. Here was another instance when my own myopic perspective was overruled.

Priority setting sometimes goes the other way. An African American student who was just starting to get involved with Amherst Christian Fellowship asked if he could meet with me. His faith had come alive during his time at Amherst, and now he wanted to make his spiritual growth a higher priority. He wondered if it would be all right to drop baseball so that he could have more time for the Fellowship and the Bi-Semester Christian Worship Series. He quit baseball and became a small group leader in the Fellowship and an influential co-chair of the Bi-Semester African American worship service.

Disciples of Christ must learn to make good decisions, selecting their priorities from many good options. Making such decisions with care and purpose is a sign of maturity and an indication that one is learning to live under the Lordship of Christ. As leaders we are tempted to confuse our role with God's role. We are right to invite people into positions of leadership, to encourage them to attend a conference, or to assist them in planning a mission trip. Challenging people to develop their gifts and serve others is a mark of good leadership. But we do not have all of the information. Christ is the head of his Body, and we are not. Ultimately, good decision-making takes place in the fear of the Lord, in prayer, and in consultation with others. Leaders have to be willing to accept a "no" reply from people and trust that, in God's sovereignty, the "foiling" of our plans can be used for good.

Some fellowships and churches emphasize one-to-one discipleship. We have tended to emphasize small groups and cluster meetings. Jesus spent almost no time alone with individual disciples. Apart from his prayer times alone with the Father, he was with the cluster of three (Peter, James and John), the twelve Apostles, the seventy, or larger groups. Individual times were brief and often for remediation, as with Peter in John 21. Such clusters, or small groups, generally make people feel less "on the spot" than one-to-one meetings. Cluster groups are also helpful in making up for one another's discipleship blind spots. In a multiethnic setting, small groups are an opportunity to learn about our histories, cultures, differences, and commonality without the higher pressure of a one-to-one meeting. This is not to denigrate one-to-one meetings, for which there is always a place. I simply mean to emphasize the benefits of small groups, particularly in cross-cultural contexts.

Leadership in a multiethnic fellowship sets the standard for relationships. The quality of relationships amongst the leaders will be reflected throughout the fellowship. If there is unity and a sense of common purpose amongst leaders, then members of the fellowship will sense that and benefit. Alternatively, if there is discord and division amongst the leaders, then the larger membership will struggle with unity. This is more than simply a human leadership principle, but it reflects a divine reality and a vital way in which the work of God's Spirit is enhanced or hindered.

Another area of challenge to a multiethnic community is our view of ontology (the nature of our being) and the atonement (Christ's reconciling humankind to God). How do we think about ourselves? How has God addressed our problems on the cross? Mako Nagasawa (Nagasawa 2001) has provided a helpful structure for thinking about these differences in a multiethnic context. He suggests that there are two major types of self-concepts. Majority American culture generally subscribes to a guilt-based model that says, "My mistakes don't define me. Though I have some problems, I'm essentially okay." The individual's response to guilt is to work at self-improvement. The guilt-based understanding of self is able to develop in majority culture where there is relational and environmental stability.

Non-westerners and American minorities often view themselves through a shame-based ontology. Nagasawa suggests that this develops from relational and environmental instability and the internalization of negative criticism and rejection. The shame-based culture thinks of the group as good but the individual as bad. The shame-based person thinks, "I have a lot of problems; I'm essentially bad. My bad character and mistakes define me" and "I have a layer of goodness that I need to project as a façade. I can't let people know who I really am."

These two views have a significant impact when we consider how they interact with the work of Christ on the cross. The white, evangelical church has largely focused on a legal, substitutionary perspective. According to this way of thinking about the atonement, Jesus died on the cross in our place to take the Father's wrath that we deserved. Jesus' died in our place so that that we no longer need to fear punishment for our sins. Sin is thought of as wrong actions and thoughts that deserve God's punishment and Christ's death on the cross dealt with sin by appeasing God's anger toward us. Most Asian American pastors were trained in majority white seminaries and so utilize the same language. But in a shame based culture the forgiveness gained on the cross may be understood not as debt-forgiveness but as debt-obligation. Rather than gaining relief from the effects of sin, the burden is shifted to the individual.

In the African American church, and in a growing number of minority churches, less emphasis is placed on the substitutionary and legal effects of Christ's work, and more emphasis placed on the relational results of the atonement, our union with Christ and our adoption as children of God. Prior to coming to faith, we were separated from God by our very nature. As believers, however, we died to our old selves (nature) with Christ on the cross and were resurrected with Christ as our new selves. We can experience the love of God for his Son as those who are transformed by Christ's work and adopted as God's children. The cross and resurrection were something we experienced with Christ, rather than a transaction completed by Christ on our behalf.

An emphasis on our relational union with Christ and our adoption will motivate us in pursuing reconciliation, understanding, and the family love of God.

Church traditions vary in worship style and conventions. Each person brings his or her own unique combination of roles – his or her own story – to the fellowship. To the extent that we are able to broaden our understanding of what each of these roles means to individuals and their ethnic groups, our community will be deepened. Similarly, to the extent that we are unfamiliar with major roles individuals hold, our community will be less authentic and relationships more on the surface.

The Venn Diagram gives an example of an individual with several overlapping roles. Others in the fellowship would have varying degrees of identification with each of these roles. Each element contributes significantly to the whole life of this person. A person's ethnic background may create quite different expectations for what it means to be a daughter, for instance, and especially a daughter with a sick and elderly parent. Likewise, being a single parent adds pressures that may not be present for two-parent families or someone who is single. All of these factors, and more, are active in the person's life when she walks through the door on a Sunday morning.

Her outside responsibilities significantly affect her availability for service or leadership responsibilities.

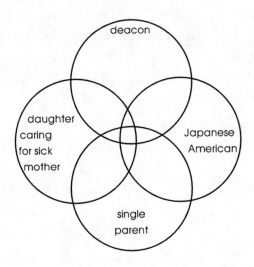

Figure 2: Venn Diagram of Roles

People of color will have varying degrees of comfort within a multi-ethnic fellowship. They are likely, particularly during the college years, to move through several shifts in understanding their own personal and ethnic identities. There may be times when it is exceedingly difficult for them to interact regularly with whites or people of other ethnicities besides their own. There may be times when it is very helpful for them to closely associate with a faith community whose membership is largely of their own ethnic make-up. We need to allow people the freedom to do this without apology, as it is a part of helping them to mature in Christ. There are things that an ethnic church or community can provide that a multiethnic fellowship cannot. Participating in such fellowships can be like "going home" and finding comfort and familiarity there. Sometimes we need that.

In the next chapter I talk about ways we can make changes in a fellowship to make it feel more comfortable for everyone.

10

RESTRUCTURING MULTIETHNIC FELLOWSHIPS

PAUL SORRENTINO

Ministry involving people of diverse ethnicities will, of necessity, differ from models that may work in more homogeneous settings. In this chapter, I make some recommendations born out of fifteen years of experience with an intentionally multiethnic fellowship. A lot of these lessons have been learned through trial and error. Many of these principles are also applicable to people who are not ethnic minorities and for a Christian community that is not multiethnic. Our point is not that these concerns relate only to multiethnic fellowships, but that they are especially important for multiethnic fellowships.

WHAT WORKS?

In his research Michael Emerson has identified several common features of healthy multiracial congregations. First, and perhaps most important, successful multiracial fellowships have leaders who are committed to seeing that the church makes changes that will allow people of diverse backgrounds to worship and serve God together. Key decision makers in the church and, the senior clergy must be involved. The key leader or leaders will need to help the church members to make sometimes difficult changes as they seek to develop a new church culture.

Becoming a multiethnic fellowship is not like adding another program to the variety of church offerings. It is an entirely different way of doing church. Who will the speakers be? What illustrations will be used in sermons? What books added to the church library? How will the music change?

Without a strong commitment on the part of leadership, the fellowship is not likely to make it through these significant adjustments. Successful multiracial congregations have a membership that is willing to make changes needed to accommodate a multiracial fellowship. This willingness is largely dependent on the persuasiveness of senior leadership (Emerson and Woo 2006, 28).

Emerson also found that two other factors, musical style and vision, correlated closely with racial diversity in a congregation. Upbeat musical style accompanied higher levels of racial diversity, and racially diverse churches often have a vision statement that explicitly states the congregation's commitment to being multiracial. These findings were consistent across the multiracial churches that seemed to be working well (Emerson and Woo 2006, 72-73).

MODELS OF INVOLVEMENT

A common ministry model of participation can be pictured in terms of concentric circles. The center circle denotes maximum participation. A person in the outermost circle may have simply expressed interest in the fellowship by signing a form during orientation, attending an event or friendship with a member. A person slightly closer to the center may attend a large group meeting or small group occasionally. Movement toward the center involves regular small group and large group attendance and may include membership in a high-commitment small group, praise team leadership, conference attendance, participation in a short-term missions project, and being part of the executive leadership team. A person generally takes on additional responsibilities and commitments as he or she moves towards the center (Figure 3).

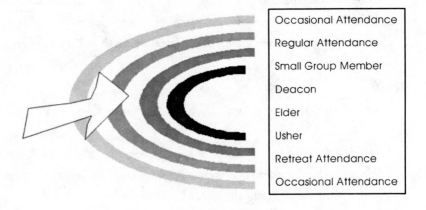

Figure 3: Concentric Circle Model

The concentric circle model is subject to misuse in two ways. First, leaders sometimes apply it inflexibly with minimal or no allowance for exceptions. It is quite possible to take a good thing and destroy it by an overly strict application. This was the error of the Pharisees. Second, this model encourages the view that heightened involvement in the fellowship or church is always better. The model conveys an implicit message that one's commitment to Christ is measured in direct proportion to one's involvement in the fellowship. The more one does with the fellowship, the more spiritual one is. I want to challenge this "more is better" assumption and, especially, the universal application of the concentric circle model to all people and situations. At Amherst we found there are significant liabilities when this model is utilized with students of color.

CORE ISSUES

The dominant culture meets many of the needs of majority whites. This frees them to engage in the activities of the concentric circles described above. Majority people are often unaware of ways that their needs are being met and consequently wonder why minorities raise so many concerns or, as is more often the case, simply "vote with their feet" and drop out of the fellowship, if they were ever involved at all.

Carl Ellis has argued that the critical issue in multiethnic relationships and ministry is an appreciation of one another's "core issues." He categorizes core issues as personal, social and cultural. Personal core issues are universal, internal reactions such as fear, loneliness, and anxiety. Social concerns include education, health, and family. While such issues are common to all people, there can be dramatic differences in the way these needs are experienced based on an individual's socio-economic, ethnic, and physical health status. Cultural core issues are variable in their expression and tend to be specific to each people group (Ellis 2001).

Many social and cultural core issues of majority people are addressed by the broader society, so they may not even need to think about them. As a result, majority people are much more likely to focus on personal core issues. Since personal core issues are common to all people, there is some attraction to these areas for people of color as well. Everyone wants to overcome anxiety and to feel relationally close to others. However, with so many other pressing needs, it is far more difficult for people of color to focus only on personal core issues.

Differing constellations of core issues mean that behaviors that appear identical on the outside have varied meanings for individuals. These meanings may not be readily apparent, particularly for those who are unaware of the differences in cultural core issues. For instance, a student with a long family tradition of college education may view studying quite differently from one coming out of a family and community where few if any members have attended college. For the former, an extreme focus on studies and grades to the exclusion of nearly everything else might be a form of academic idolatry. For the latter, a determined effort to focus on studies might be good stewardship of their education. Some students may indeed represent their entire community back home. This representative responsibility carried by a minority student may weigh heavily on the student in a way that a majority student would have difficulty understanding. Outward behaviors may look the same to the casual observer, but the background context makes their meaning entirely different.

People of color may need to be involved in ethnic-specific groups and activities for which whites have little interest or need. Some of these activities may relate to central aspects of a person's identity. A black student who has grown up in a predominantly black community may find it important to her spiritual and emotional health to be involved in a black church and the Black Student Union on campus. These activities speak to who she is in a way that a multiethnic Christian group simply cannot. A Korean American student may find the "conversational prayer" style of the majority church stifling and passionless. It may be important for him or her to be with other Korean Americans in a more choral style of prayer. In the concentric circle model, people of color who want to be committed to a multiethnic fellowship may be placed in the uncomfortable position where, in order to be more deeply involved, they would have to reduce or eliminate ties with groups that better meet their social and cultural core issues. This creates a basic identity tension that majority people are simply not required to address.

I attended a Kwanzaa celebration where a highly respected member of the college's administration called upon members of the black community to make certain commitments. She is an African American Christian woman, and the requests she made were all good and reasonable. They were things that would strengthen the black community on campus and that would make each student's parents proud. However, they would all require payment of that most precious of commodities, time.

When people of color are asked to take on time-demanding responsibilities within their own ethnic communities or churches, these may well conflict with expectations of the Christian fellowship. These people may then be called upon to make fundamental loyalty decisions that go to the core of their being. Are they black or Christian? No one should have to face that kind of artificial choice. The Christian group that causes them to do that is creating an unnecessary and painful marginalization of people of color. Similarly, a member may wish to attend a Bible study at a Chinese church instead of the small group on campus or at the multiracial church. In general, these situations should be seen as opportunities to support our brothers and sisters of color and their well-being rather than competition with the agenda of our own fellowship.

ELLIPSES MODEL

Rather than a model that encourages people to hit the concentric circle bull's-eye, we need a model that not only allows, but even encourages, involvement in multiple spheres. I find it helpful to think in terms of ellipses of involvement (Figure 4).

This is a much messier diagram than the concentric circle model. However, it more accurately reflects how people experience life and ministry. An ellipse is an oblong with two fixed points or foci. The two foci have a major axis connecting them, like a subway line between two destinations. A man comes to a church leaders' meeting. He then returns to his home to take his son to his violin lesson. The next day he goes to work, drops by church to meet with the pastor and then goes to an Urban League meeting. On the weekend, he spends time on a Habitat for Humanity build, goes home to make dinner with his wife, and they attend a special missions conference at church. Real life requires constant traversing between multiple points. The "ellipses of involvement" model recognizes the complexity of life and the responsibility for the fellowship to help its members live godly lives in light of all of those various foci.

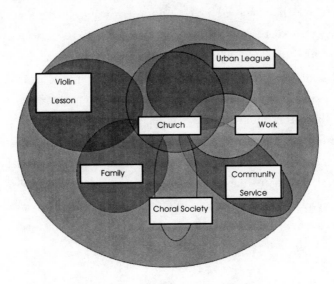

Figure 4: Ellipses of Involvement

The church should not be a place that supports the bifurcation of life, but its integration. Life in the kingdom of God is all-encompassing. It is not divided into my "Christian" activities and my "other" activities. Being a disciple of Jesus involves all that we do, not only those activities done within the confines of formal fellowship structures, in accordance with Paul's instructions in Colossians: "And whatever you do, whether in word or deed, do it all in the name of the Lord Jesus, giving thanks to God the Father through him" (Col. 3:17).

The various commitments that the members of a multiethnic fellowship have should be objects of prayer, support, and, where helpful, training. The community of faith must live with a conscious awareness of what happens outside of its own particular activities, for these too are places for kingdom work.

This approach makes leadership and discipleship more challenging. The goal is no longer to maximize involvement in the fellowship, but to help people to live a life of faith wherever they are and in whatever they are doing. Expectations for fellowship involvement must be adaptable, depending on the needs, particular time in life (both age and the calendar), gifting, and availability of fellowship members. If a leader has a sick family member, then his or her responsibilities should be reduced to allow the person to go home on weekends or whenever needed. When students have comprehensive exams coming up, they should have the option of minimizing other commitments while they prepare.

One danger of this approach may seem to be over-commitment – simply too many foci in one's life. I would contend that this is just as easily the case with other models, perhaps even more so because extra-fellowship activities may not be taken into consideration. The bottom line is that life in the Christian community must be about learning to make good and responsible decisions with the recognition that Christ is the Lord. Leaders and friends must always be helping one another to ascertain God's will in light of competing demands. Whenever possible, major decisions should be made in consultation with other believers the individual respects. Decision-making under the lordship of Christ is an invaluable life-skill. It provides the opportunity to expand one's trust in God and is a mark of a maturing disciple.

We must hold our own agendas lightly. Leaders might encourage and invite people to come to a retreat, work in the nursery, be a deacon, or to lead a small group. If the person says "no" for good reasons, then this should become an opportunity to rejoice in all that God is doing and not to lay on a guilt trip.

At a recent InterVarsity retreat I would have loved to have seen a large turnout from Amherst Christian Fellowship. The speaker was excellent, and I know the value of taking a break from normal routine. I did not realize how many conflicting events were scheduled for that same weekend. One of my volunteer staff, a youth minister at a local church, had asked some Fellowship members to help him with his first major youth meeting that Saturday. It was the weekend of "the biggest little football game in the country," Amherst College's annual battle with Williams College, drawing away football players and band members. A dance recital and a musical performance involved more of our members. A women's retreat at one of the local churches attracted many in the fellowship. And it was mid-term exam time.

The net result was a dozen or so Christian Fellowship members at the weekend retreat. I would have liked more, but I was thankful that most of those not there chose to do something else for good reasons — reasons that we have been trying to teach as part of what it means to be members of a fellowship committed to one another and heirs together of life in Christ. We have encouraged our members to support one another by attending each other's events whenever possible. I was glad that people chose to support one another rather than just attend an event.

SOME GUIDING PRINCIPLES

Our guidelines concerning fellowship involvement are intended to help people maintain a healthy balance of time usage in the various spheres to which God has called them. First, we seldom select first-year students for major, formal leadership positions. They may well be capable, and have quite possibly held significant positions in youth group or its equivalent before, but we want them to have a year to adjust to the demands of college life without added responsibilities. For many high-powered students, it actually takes some doing to get them to the place of allowing themselves to be served rather than always serving. We do, however, want them to quickly be in a place where they can contribute in some way to the life of the community.

Second, students should generally have no more than two official leadership responsibilities in the Fellowship. They may be on the worship team and lead the outreach team. Or, they may lead prayer meetings and a small group. Two leadership responsibilities seems to be the maximum level of involvement most students or church volunteers can handle well while still being able to pray and dream about their role and still pay proper attention to the other foci in their life. This is not a fixed rule, but an average. Some people can do more, some less. The guiding principle is that leadership should be good for people. Our aim is to have people see leadership as a benefit to them and a gift from God rather than feeling manipulated, burned out, used and resentful toward other leaders or, worse, God.

Third, it is good for people to have something in their life that takes them beyond their comfort zone and requires that they trust in God and not simply their own abilities. The goal here, as another staff worker once told me, is to stretch people "so much that they fall on their knees, but not so much that they fall on their face."

A central goal of our community is to help individuals, especially Christian leaders, to ascertain God's direction and will for their lives while still keeping in mind the wider needs of the Christian Fellowship. Where will a person grow the most in his or her faith? Where will he or she have the most influence for God's kingdom? What are the current needs of the fellowship that may fit with this particular person? We as leaders must recognize in practice what we declare in doxology: Jesus is Lord. God's plans for someone may differ from our own.

FAITH IN ACTION

On the night that the police arrested Rosa Parks in Montgomery, Alabama, leaders began making telephone calls. The next night, black ministers and professionals met and planned the famous boycott of Montgomery's segregated bus system. They met at Dexter Avenue Baptist Church, where the Reverend Dr. Martin Luther King, Jr. was the minister.

Dr. King led an entire community in an effective response against injustice by connecting faith in God and concern for the lost with social concern and action. He preached that "any religion that professes to be concerned with the souls of men and is not concerned with the slums that damn them and the social conditions that cripple them, is a dry-as-dust religion"(Shuker 1985, 47).

Many churches and fellowships have become "dry-as-dust religion" for lack of a whole person and whole society concern. This is seldom by design, but often by default as our programs and commitments leave no room for action or involvement outside of the bounds of our own church or fellowship. "Faith by itself," James says, "if it is not accompanied by action, is dead"(James 2:17). While this is true for all Christians, it is even more critical for multiethnic fellowships to demonstrate faith in Christ by our deeds.

The black church has had a long history of reflecting its faith by involvement in the community. The white evangelical majority church, by contrast, has sometimes said the right things, but avoided what might appear to be "social justice" involvement for fear of appearing to be like the socially conscious but theologically liberal church. People have reason to question the legitimacy of faith that they hear spoken but do not see lived out. Putting our faith into practice lends credibility to our talk and helps us to walk as Jesus walked.

In the Sermon on the Mount Jesus emphasized the importance of applying what we learn:

> *Therefore everyone who hears these words of mine and puts them into practice is like a wise man who built his house on the rock. The rain came down, the streams rose, and the winds blew and beat against that house; yet it did not fall, because it had its foundation on the rock. But everyone who hears these words of mine and does not put them into practice is like a foolish man who built his house on sand. The rain came down, the streams rose, and the winds blew and beat against that house, and it fell with a great crash* (Matt. 7:24-27).

Similarly, in his upper room discourse Jesus told his disciples that their experience of the love of God would actually be enhanced and deepened when they obeyed his teaching: "If anyone loves me, he will obey my teaching. My Father will love him, and we will come to him and make our home with him." (John 14:23)

While we do talk about "application" in our small groups and sermons, we often get so caught up in our good programs that members have little time to put their faith into practice outside of the church. What Martin Luther King, Jr. did in Montgomery was not just an act that helped to alleviate suffering, but a powerful act of discipleship as he helped people to apply Christ's teachings directly to an immediate crisis.

While not neglecting teaching, musical worship, prayer and individual devotions, we must move our teaching and devotion into action. Rick Warren of Saddleback Church has called for a second reformation. The first reformation dealt with creeds, but the second must deal with deeds (Boorstein 2008).

Belief does matter. We make scripture the basis for our messages at church and in our small groups. We teach the creeds so that people have some points of reference and continuity with brothers and sisters throughout the ages. However, our beliefs must be lived out, validated, and deepened through what we do. Ours must be a faith in action.

The Urbana 2000 Student Missions Convention echoed this priority in a repeated emphasis that worship leads to mission and mission leads to worship. Our doxology heightens our desire to respond in obedience and our service deepens our doxology.

PRAYER & PRAISE

A multiethnic worship gathering awaits us in heaven. In Revelation the Apostle John describes his vision of heavenly worship:

> After this I looked and there before me was a great multitude that no-one could count, from every nation, tribe, people and language, standing before the throne and in front of the Lamb. They were wearing white robes and were holding palm branches in their hands. And they cried in a loud voice:
>
> "Salvation belongs to our God,
>
> who sits on the throne,
>
> and to the Lamb" (Rev. 7:9-10).

If we are to begin to experience such worship on earth, we will need God's intervention. Racial healing is a complex process. Corporate and individual history may smolder within individuals in a multiethnic fellowship. Many issues are so personal that they are largely unknown to others and may be hidden even to the individual affected by them. Further, the enemy of our souls seems to attack any attempt by believers to unite. Racial reconciliation has proven to be a powerful battleground. We dare not attempt it in our own strength. Genuine love for one another is so challenging that Jesus said it would mark people as his disciples. Jesus concluded his upper room discourse with a prayer for his disciples' unity (John 13:34-35; 17:20-26).

Prayer and worship present particular challenge to a multiethnic fellowship, and these challenges are addressed more fully in chapter 12. Singing and prayer are central to how we experience God. If we are to come together in prayer and worship, we must learn from one another in humility. We must see our own style of prayer and singing as one style among many rather than the preferred or "normal" style. Throughout eternity, we will never become bored with the multi-faceted diamond of prayer and praise. Robert Webber defines worship as "a community response to the God who has acted in history" (Webber 2000). Learning to respond to God in ways that are meaningful to all its members will provide rich rewards for a multiethnic community.

Effective prayer for healing from the evils of racism will be costly prayer. The Reverend Dr. Alice Brown-Collins has suggested that "Lift Every Voice and Sing," usually referred to as The Black or Negro National Anthem, serves as a model prayer for African Americans (Brown-Collins 2000). The final stanza of the anthem petitions:

> God of our weary years, God of our silent tears,
> Thou who hast brought us thus far on the way;
> Thou who hast by Thy might led us into the light,
> Keep us forever in the path, we pray.
> Lest our feet stray from the places, our God, where we met Thee,
> Lest our hearts, drunk with the wine of the world, we forget Thee,
> Shadowed beneath Thy hand, may we forever stand,
> True to our God, true to our native land (Johnson and Johnson 1970).

Not only African Americans, but all ethnic groups, come with their own stories of how God has led them thus far. Each of those stories needs to be heard and valued if we are to develop the kind of Christ-centered community that exhibits a genuine love for one another, the kind that shows us to be his disciples. In heaven, we will have unlimited time for listening, prayer, and praise. We might as well get a head start.

11
LEADERS OF A MULTIETHNIC FELLOWSHIP
SARAH BASS & JANET LYDECKER
WITH JENN ROBERGE CHUDY, ROB GODZENO, JANET HA,
BONNIE LIN AND MATT MASCIOLI

College is the stage of development when most young adults are first exposed to other people who may share a similar goal, but come from varied backgrounds. For the seven students who eventually came to serve together on the Fellowship's leadership team for 1-2 years, Amherst embodied this experience of sharing a common goal and encountering individuals from diverse cultural backgrounds—racially, ethnically, geographically, politically, socially, religiously, and in many other ways. But the seven students who served together on the Fellowship's leadership team found themselves called to go beyond the typical exposure to diversity college students receive. Instead, through an examination of personal experiences, convictions, biases and prejudices, community building and conflict resolution, they learned firsthand what it means to be leaders of an authentically multiethnic Christian body.

Some models of racial development map out a trajectory of how individuals come to embrace their own racial identity, and how that identity influences their worldview (e.g., Helms 1995). This process involves movement from naïve unawareness of race, to an active advocacy for race-focused social justice. The goal of race-focused social justice is to embrace diverse ethnic backgrounds, and actively work towards a society that equally values all individuals. For members of the majority, white Americans, this means that we must become aware of areas where we hold privilege and actively fight against taking that privilege away from individuals in racial minorities. For racial minorities in America, this means working to claim authority and power despite not having race-based privilege and actively educating individuals from racial minorities and majorities about egalitarian treatment.

As racial consciousness develops, individuals grow to be influenced by socialization, learn to resist prejudiced attitudes from this socialization, feel guilt for having believed these attitudes, and move towards defining and internalizing a new, more positive and inclusive racial identity (Helms 1995). The Amherst Christian Fellowship was a place that fostered the re-evaluation and reconstruction of members' identities and definitions of self in a way new to many of them. As a result of the conciliatory initiative to make the Fellowship a deliberately diverse community of believers, especially along racial and ethnic lines, ideas and beliefs about race emerged as a significant factor for most members, warranting more consideration than had been necessary in many of their past experiences. By the time students graduated, however, many who remained committed came to internalize the value and necessity of embracing others from different backgrounds, not for the sake of political correctness, but because they had become aware of the vitality of difference to the strength, unity and effectiveness in of the body of Christ.

Our leadership team included seven people. Matt is a white man from Morgantown, West Virginia. Rob is a white student from Connecticut. Janet H., ethnically Korean American, was born while her parents were studying for their doctorates at the University of Chicago and baptized as a little girl in a church community of Korean graduate students. Jenn, a white, Massachusetts native, knew no more than two dozen people who were not white prior to attending college. Janet L. is also a white woman from Massachusetts. Bonnie is a Chinese American woman from New Jersey. And Sarah is an African American woman from West Chicago, Illinois.

Sarah did not have any spiritual expectations coming to Amherst. Hailing from the suburban Midwest, she recognized Amherst as a majority white school, and therefore expected the fellowship to reflect majority culture in its community. Though her background had made her accustomed to the culture of conservative, evangelical white Christians, she says she always felt peripheral in that environment because the community tended to be insular, cliquish and xenophobic. Sarah recalls encountering an unexpected surprise when she met the Fellowship's religious advisor.

> I remember walking into my first Friday Night Fellowship, knowing no one. I stood in the lounge, nervously nibbling a cookie when I was suddenly confronted with a kind, smiling face and an outstretched hand. I shook it as Paul introduced himself, warmly welcoming me to the Fellowship. He then began talking about his vision for the Fellowship, and how that vision was centered on racial reconciliation and a multiethnic community. He continued to talk about various networks for students of color, and ways I could find racial and cultural support within the body of Christ.

Paul's perspective surprised Sarah. Not only did his words express his consideration and appreciation for her experience as a person of color she recognized him as the only white man she had ever met in a Christian setting who reached out to her first, making it less of a sacrifice for her to reach back.

Reaching out to white individuals can be a sacrifice in part because past, negative memories of interactions with other white individuals can resurface. Bonnie, a Chinese American woman from New Jersey, felt the lasting impact of racial marginalization that she carried from childhood. "When I was in seventh grade," she recounted, "a group of kids cast pennies and racial slurs at me in the school cafeteria while shouting 'go back to Ellis Island' and 'go find some better clothes at the Salvation Army.' Disconcerting as it was, this was neither the first nor the last time I would experience discrimination on account of race." Bonnie grew up in South Brunswick, a multicultural community with a large South Asian population, as well as African American, white, and Latino individuals. There, one could find several Christian churches, the Chabad Jewish Center, the Islamic Society of Central Jersey, and the Hindu Durga Temple. She described having childhood friends who wore headscarves and prayed in a special room at noon, friends who watched Bollywood movies and wore bright saris to parties, and friends who celebrated Passover Seders and took weekly night classes in Hebrew.

Despite the racially diverse community in which she grew up, Bonnie attended a predominantly Chinese nondenominational church throughout her childhood and youth. "Although I abstractly agreed that it's a pity that 11 o'clock on a Sunday morning is the most racially segregated hour in the United States," she said, "I never really thought that I was part of that picture." Like other immigrant churches, her home church in Princeton attracted many newcomers and international students from East Asia because it provided a safe space to worship in a familiar style, in a familiar language, and with familiar-looking people. This was a great comfort to those navigating an unfamiliar and sometimes intolerant world.

There was loveliness in worshipping with people who shared a common ethnicity, but the Christian Fellowship opened her eyes to the sublime beauty in worshipping the same God with different peoples. "This did not happen overnight," she clarified at one point, "I confess I found the Fellowship's worship style slightly creepy at first. The band seemed a little strange, often picking unusual songs in Spanish or Creole, and keeping beat with a mean set of bongos. Some people had an inordinate fancy for clapping and hand gestures. Others liked to interrupt prayers with passionate expressions of 'Hallelujah!' or 'Amen!'" This was a significant change from the general worship experience at her home church. She grew to learn that the Fellowship, and the Body of Christ, is about more than worship style.

The academic community was particularly suited to giving the students who would eventually become leaders a head start on the process of understanding the importance of an intentionally multiethnic fellowship. Many of them chose to go to Amherst because of its diversity, commitment to a broader understanding of the world and attention to issues of social justice. What few were expecting was how much these same values were necessary in Christian fellowship. They entered into a fellowship committed to unity in love across ethnic and denominational differences, and an appreciation of those differences. Just like the college of which it was a part, membership in the Fellowship was a training-ground in helping students become better servants of Christ in the future. The Fellowship's racial and ethnic diversity, and the recognition and celebration of those differences in the expression of faith, presented members and leaders with wonderful opportunities to grow in Christ. It helped build strong relationships with fellow Christians through the triumphs and the shortcomings, raising up future leaders of multiethnic communities and in missions.

The experience of being part of an intentionally multiethnic fellowship became central to the cultural identities of many of members, pushing them along the continuum of their development as multiethnic leaders. Serving as a member of a multiethnic student leadership team presented both benefits and challenges. It offered the leaders the chance to be discipled in a small setting and to be servant leaders. Having multiple cultural perspectives proved very important. The leaders came to recognize the responsibility, commitment and concentration required to maintain the level of racial and cultural consciousness necessary for a welcoming community across racial and ethnic lines. Leaders of color needed to be active in offering input when leadership decisions were made; likewise, white leaders needed to be regularly challenged to assess a situation or decision from multiple angles that they may not have considered previously, taking into account the potential impact on different groups of people.

A conflict that arose during a time of transition for the Fellowship was a shaping experience for the leadership team. One African American woman, raised in a relatively homogeneous fellowship of Eritrean believers in a predominantly African American neighborhood in Chicago, was invited to be part of the Fellowship's student leadership team. This student got involved in the Fellowship at the beginning of her freshman year at Amherst, co-founding a group called B.A.S.I.C. (Brothers And Sisters In Christ), an accountability group geared toward African and African American believers on campus. She was dedicated to the ministry of students of color from the very beginning, as demonstrated by her efforts. She loved the Lord and actively served in the Fellowship where help was needed. Her conviction and commitment, therefore, made her an easy and desirable candidate for the leadership team.

As the current African American student on the leadership team, Sarah chose to talk to this student about the leadership position invitation. When approached, this student met the offer with a great deal of hesitation. She told Sarah that despite her involvement in the Fellowship she did not feel entirely comfortable around the white members of the community. Not only did they worship differently, but she found that they made little effort to reach out to racial minority students. She said that racial minorities already feel significant discomfort walking into the weekly service or a Fellowship Bible study and being in the minority. That discomfort is intensified by the discomfort of feeling forced to have to keep to themselves because members of the white majority could hide in their numbers, choosing neither to compromise nor confront the discomfort racial minorities felt in a cultural setting so decidedly different from their own. No African American student wants to take that on, she explained.

In spite of her reservations, this student eventually agreed to join the leadership team on a trial basis. Not long into the transition, however, she decided to leave. Her sudden resignation upset many of the other leaders, including Paul Sorrentino, the team advisor. Everyone sensed that there was an issue at hand, but no one knew how to go about fixing it, and this student offered no explanation for her decision. Paul eventually asked Sarah if she would be willing to talk to this student about her concerns, and ask what needed to be changed and whether a resolution could be reached that would bring her back to the leadership team. Sarah agreed, and when she sat down with her and got into conversation, this student began to reiterate many of the initial concerns she had when contemplating the position.

Her concerns troubled Paul. He felt that they needed to be promptly addressed in front of the whole Fellowship. Rather than ask this student to articulate her personal frustrations, however, he asked Sarah to take the time at a large group meeting to share her own experience with the community and to talk about the real challenges facing many students of color. The goal was to communicate to members of the Fellowship the importance of cultural sensitivity in a society established on racial and ethnic divisions. The hope was that every member would therefore be compelled to avoid replicating those divisions and move instead towards reconciliation.

Sarah shared her background with the college Fellowship and spoke frankly about the anger and hurt associated with exclusion, especially in the body of Christ where Christians are called to a different way of life. She explained that racial reconciliation called for everyone to give a little of themselves and take a little discomfort for the sake of unity. Believers truly committed to the Kingdom of God will recognize the importance of being to others like Jesus of Nazareth and also Simon of Cyrene, in not only taking up their daily crosses, but also helping their brothers and sisters shoulder theirs.

This was not an easy shift for white student leaders for a number of reasons, despite their willingness and commitment to creating and sustaining a multiethnic Christian community. White students, like students of color, do not always share the same cultural experiences. One student admitted to struggling with the issue of race both as a member and leader of a multiethnic fellowship, acknowledging her own initial lack of desire to compromise her comfort for the sake of others, despite recognizing the fact that students with different cultures and traditions often do it regularly. Only later did she begin to come to terms with the fact that one cannot be an effective leader in a diverse fellowship by simply doing what feels most comfortable for the individual. One of the greatest challenges was how to make different aspects of the Fellowship more accessible to people from different backgrounds. She describes feeling as though she had nothing to say as a white student, having a racial background that was practically homogeneous, and having no real experiences of multiracial interaction until arriving at college. She explained, however, that serving on the leadership team and listening to others debate various topics, such as how to enhance individuals' ability to worship, taught her to respect different backgrounds as part of the individual and engage in these important issues, for the wholeness of a community is established in the coming together of its unique parts.

That meeting was a turning point for the Fellowship. Out of it came one of the most genuine conversations Christians of different racial and ethnic backgrounds had ever had with each other at Amherst. Members talked about their backgrounds and perspectives on the role of racial diversity and reconciliation within a fellowship, and out of those conversations, visible efforts began to be made by all towards greater unity. The student who had initially expressed her discomfort ended up rejoining the leadership team that semester and found the atmosphere improved.

The Fellowship's struggle to become one in the body of Christ did not end there. Unity is dynamic and requires committed engagement for the long term. The challenge continues, as it did before, and as it will hereafter. Anything worth having requires sacrifice. The struggle, however, is necessary for the beauty of what comes of it: compassion, mercy, and ready forgiveness. It is hard, it is painful, and it is frustrating. It is what Jesus meant when he said, "Follow me."

Being effective leaders in a multiethnic fellowship required individuals to keep the experiences of others in mind while being aware of the significance of their own experience in the shaping of their identities. This is not always easy. To form a family out of any group of people is difficult enough, let alone when one adds the variables of background, ethnicity and tradition. All individuals must question themselves and come to terms with their own biases and prejudices during the process, evaluating and openly sharing the ways in which background and ethnicity shape perspectives and worldviews. A community of trust, however, is required for everyone in a fellowship to feel greater freedom in exchanging personal sentiments for the sake of working through concerns, growing closer as individuals and edifying the collective body. The dialogues that unfold in a fellowship community of trust prove fruitful, for members can constructively be made aware of the neglect they can unwittingly impose on each other, and be challenged to readily forgive offenses and love fellow believers through their mistakes and imperfections. Believers learn firsthand that the burdens of one become the burden of all in a truly Christ-centered community of mercy and love.

Serving as leaders in a multiethnic fellowship has had enduring influence on the personal and professional lives of many of the students after college. Many graduated having adopted participation in multiethnic, multidenominational community as a personal value. Several of the former leaders have gone on to do missions and volunteer work in diverse areas; some continued to intentionally seek out friendships and communities of individuals with ethnicities from all walks of life; others chose to marry individuals from different cultural backgrounds; one former leader celebrates having served on a pastoral search committee that has led to the calling of the church's first African American pastor in the church's 370 year history. Most leaders give credit to the experiences they had in an intentionally multiethnic fellowship for opening their minds to these possibilities and committing them to service and social justice as outflows of their faith in the Gospel. Yet while the lessons learned as leaders in the Amherst Christian Fellowship have led individuals to actively seek out intentionally multiethnic faith communities and labor on behalf of the marginalized, they recognized that multiethnic fellowship demands lifelong commitment, engagement, participation and compassion. Everyone has blind spots, making community with brothers and sisters from every tribe, language, people and nation necessary to the embodiment of the Kingdom of God, united by a common Savior and King.

Although believers display many external differences, from skin color to denominational background, all are the beloved adopted children of the Heavenly Father; the Holy Spirit dwelling in the Catholic biology major who only prays in Korean, also dwells in the warm-hearted Haitian who bursts into song in the middle of her speech, the straight-up white athlete from West Virginia, the mischievous Puerto Rican from the Bronx, the jazz-loving Mexican Indian who dances like a fiend, and the sassy Ghanaian whose response to every misfortune in life is "Hey, at least I'm not dead." In multiethnic fellowship, whether on a college campus on in a church community, one learns that it is not external determinants, like skin color, that bind us together, but rather the internal, eternal truth that we are all running the Race together. We can have unity in diversity because regardless of where we come from, it is in God we trust. Indeed.

12

Multiethnic worship

Jacob Maguire and Julian Michael
with Melody Ko Lin and Lisa Pistorio

Imagine yourself outside on a cold, windy night. You have been trudging through the snow for miles, but you haven't seen another person since you started your journey. Your feet are cold; your face is raw. All you want is to find a warm place to thaw out and feel like yourself again. Suddenly, a dark outline appears in the distance— the silhouette of a small cottage with smoke rising from the chimney. As you make your way closer, you hear laughter and cheerful voices. You stumble to the window and rub a small hole in the frost, eager to peer inside.

Dim lamps cast a soft glow on deep, wood-paneled walls. Light emanates from a roaring fire crackling in the brick hearth. Around the fireplace, people relax comfortably. Some lie on the soft carpet, gazing meditatively at the flames. Others sit casually on couches and overstuffed chairs, chatting with friends they seem to have known forever. A few sip steaming mugs of cocoa, or maybe cider. On the mantle, you notice photographs of these same people, their arms draped around one another as they smile brightly back at you from another moment in time.

Any one of us would be thrilled to find a place like this. As humans, we long for a warm and relaxed environment, a safe place where our needs can be met in community. Perhaps, we have even experienced this type of environment in a church or college fellowship. But what if the very things that made us so comfortable in these settings also kept others from finding their way inside? What if there were people in our lives who, after arriving in our Christian communities, could only watch our experiences longingly through the window? Could it be that our "cottages" only stay so warm because we have locked the doors?

This is how one student, Lisa, described her first worship experience in her campus fellowship group. As a Roman Catholic from an Italian household, she struggled to adjust to an informal protestant worship service in college—from a full choir to a "praise team," from an organ to an electric guitar. "From the outside, the musical style and Protestant lingo took a long while to get used to," she said. "Even if they had played one song I was familiar with, I would have felt like I was on the inside, rather than perpetually on the outside."

Lisa's story is not unusual. Her sense of isolation is common in churches and fellowships across America. In the same fellowship Lisa attended, an Asian American student reported confusion and frustration at hearing songs that she knew played in styles she did not recognize. A white student shared Lisa's complaint that most of the songs he had grown up with were not played at all. An African American student confessed strong discomfort because, in his words, "Few people looked like me, and almost no one sang or prayed the way I did."

Music is among the most personal and charged elements of any worship service. It is one of the "cottage doors" that either welcomes us in or locks us out of authentic fellowship. Its variation across racial, cultural and generational lines can be both a blessing and an obstacle for church unity. As worshipers, we grow comfortable and attentive when we are familiar with music in a church setting. But when we hear songs and styles that we fail to recognize, the space around us can turn threatening or unfamiliar. We may even experience worship as an anxious struggle to fit in, rather than a time of true spiritual and emotional openness. Building authentic, multiethnic community requires that we overcome these challenges, but doing so requires shared sacrifice and informed commitment from worship leaders and the congregations they serve.

Colleges and universities offer a special place to begin this process because they bring together students from diverse backgrounds to worship together in one place. In that sense, college students may be uniquely equipped to lead the Church toward the Biblical vision of a people built from every nation, tribe, language and people. (Rev. 14:6) But how can students use the lessons they learn in this laboratory experience to help move the broader church toward a multiethnic vision after they graduate? And what can the rest of us do in our own worship settings to "catch the wave" that so many of our brothers and sisters in college have already begun to ride?

This chapter's insights on music and worship reflect the experiences of one group of college graduates who led worship together in a multiethnic college fellowship over a six-year period. Those students struggled publicly—often in front of microphones—with the unique questions and struggles that multiethnic worship presents. Out of their enduring commitment to praise and to each other grew an authentic model for worship in a multiethnic setting. Today, that model offers hope for churches and fellowship groups seeking to live out the diversity of Christ's body in a practical way.

In college, turnover is a major problem. Each year brings a new crop of first-year students with fresh energy and ideas, but it also brings the departure of the seniors who have experienced and invested in the fellowship's vision for the longest period of time. To maintain enthusiasm and broad commitment to the goal of multiethnicity, worship leaders must reassess their vision for worship and recommunicate it to their peers every year.

In churches, the variables are often different. Turnover may be less of a problem, but a long-established membership often proves just as challenging. A true commitment to multiethnicity requires structural changes to the way a church worships and often includes the introduction of new and unfamiliar musical styles. Longtime members of all ages may wonder whether this is necessary; others may voice resentment or even seek another church home. It is precisely because music is such a personal part of worship that it has the potential to create this powerful level of unease. For this reason no church can pursue multiethnicity without addressing music successfully.

Everyone has a cultural background, and each of us has been shaped by our racial and cultural realities. We may not always be conscious of this process, but we all bring racially and culturally formed identities to our places of worship. Spiritually, worship allows us to transcend our differences by encountering God together, but socially, it also offers us a cultural haven. Whether we know it or not, how we relate to God has as much to do with our cultural ties as it does with who God is and how he operates. Consequently, styles of prayer, praise and worship, and expressions of faith vary dramatically from one ethnic group to another.

These differences can be difficult to bridge because they both reflect and grow out of our culturally specific needs and expectations. Most people come to a faith community with deep, personal needs. For minority worshipers those needs often extend beyond the religious sphere. Specifically, they may seek out a place that affirms their traditions and offers them a sense of cultural belonging—a community that gives them a voice. Majority worshipers do not typically look for these elements in a church or fellowship because much of society is already arranged to fit comfortably with their cultural experiences.

Multiethnic fellowship requires that majority and minority cultures gather together in worship, but often this leads to tension that can be difficult to manage. Most of us prefer to worship in our own musical styles because these provide an intimate and familiar pathway for accessing God. New styles and traditions may confuse us or make us uncomfortable at the very moment when we long to feel settled and at home. This distrust or distaste for the unfamiliar is among the largest barriers to a cohesive and effective praise experience, and is the largest reason that the Church remains among the most unofficially segregated institutions in America.

How can a praise team honor distinct cultural needs and experiences while still creating an atmosphere that fosters unity and emphasizes Christ? What are the benefits of a racially and culturally diverse community of worship, and do they really outweigh the pain and inconvenience it takes to build one? Successful multiethnic worship ministries must grapple with these difficult questions together. Only then can they lead their congregations into effective and authentic multiethnic worship.

BUILDING AN EFFECTIVE MUSIC TEAM

Once a church or fellowship commits to multiethnicity, it must evaluate each aspect of its existing worship experience. Some things are common across almost all multiethnic fellowships—the use of songs from diverse racial and cultural traditions, for example—but many groups are reluctant to consider more structural aspects of worship, like the composition of the worship team. Worship leaders and musicians are among the most public faces in a church community, and it can be difficult to feel at ease if none of them looks like you, speaks your language or knows how to play your songs. Even in a largely homogenous church, racial, cultural and generational diversity on stage can create a climate of freedom and send a powerful visual signal that all are welcome in God's house.

A diverse praise team membership can also maximize a church's worship resources. As musicians begin to incorporate new styles and traditions into their worship repertoire, it helps to have someone in the group who is familiar with each new type of music. The technical differences between organ music and Gospel piano are enormous, for example, and even the most experienced practitioners will need help to transition from one to the other. No one should expect songs to be perfect, but members of the congregation will know if the music team has approached their respective traditions with insufficient care and attention. A team with a breadth of backgrounds and experiences can go a long way toward welcoming a diverse congregation with an authentically multiethnic sound.

For these reasons, when a church decides to pursue multiethnicity, members of the existing worship team should prayerfully consider the addition of new members with diverse backgrounds and skills. Members of the congregation should also be invited to consider how they might contribute to the ongoing work of praise. The goal here is not to "round out" the praise team by filling imaginary racial, cultural or generational quotas. Rather, it is to ask whether God might bring new faces into the ministry of worship and to offer congregants an opportunity to reflect on the role of worship in facilitating diverse fellowship. This conversation is also an excellent chance for the worship and pastoral teams to educate the congregation on the Biblical case for multiethnicity and to solicit buy-in from church members.

Once the praise team has an established membership, its members should also commit to working together without conditions. In many communities, the only criterion for being a member of the team is the desire to praise God, which means that members with significant musical and/or leadership experience may play alongside those with nothing but enthusiasm and a desire to serve. Whatever the conditions or qualifications for membership, God intends to use everyone's gifts for his glory, and members must make a commitment to serving him as one body, regardless of skill or experience level. No single member is more important than any other—God is building them all into a cohesive picture of his diverse body that the congregation can learn from and emulate.

At the same time, every good team needs a leader. This need not be the person with the most musical ability, but rather someone who is comfortable guiding the community and overseeing the efforts of the team. A good leader will solicit advice from the entire worship team, have a vision for how each practice session and service should function, and be a humble and accountable servant. He or she should also be sensitive and responsive to the multiethnic dynamic of the fellowship body, just as the Apostles were responsive to the needs of early Greek speaking believers when they were treated inequitably by Hebrew speaking believers. (Acts 6:1-6) Rotating leadership may be one way to make sure that everyone's background is well represented and that all members of the team are encouraged to take responsibility for the team's effectiveness and longevity.

The team can also grow together through the shared and democratic study of scripture. By using small blocks of practice time to discuss God's word together, members gain an opportunity to hear and respond to one another's diverse and often unexpected perspectives. This can produce greater understanding over time and increase members' sensitivity to the needs and expectations of their colleagues. By joining together over scripture, team members can begin to develop a shared vision for worship that will help to clarify team goals and the roles of individual participants over time.

The most important element of a successful multiethnic worship team is a strong focus on God as the object and center of worship. Each member of the team must abandon his or her ego and recognize that everyone on the team has chosen to be there because he or she has a heart for worship and a desire to use his or her talents to praise the Lord. No worship tradition is superior to another, and team members should learn to seek God in the varied musical and liturgical styles of their colleagues. This will often be uncomfortable, but God is the creator of culture and heritage and is pleased when his worshippers come to Him in diverse ways. We seek reconciliation not because it is edifying or even moral, but because it is God's pleasure and a sign of his character. As children of a triune God, we are born of both unity and difference. Therefore, we must be willing to make sacrifices that enable our brothers and sisters and that draw us together in praise.

This road is not a smooth one. Like all collaborative efforts, praise worship teams must experience conflict, compromise, and trial and error. Given the issues that face a multiethnic team, problems will inevitably arise regarding tempo, style, language instrumentation and song selection. It is important to approach these conflicts candidly, but with respect, always remembering that the team's success ultimately depends on a conscious choice to move beyond individual traditions and join in worship. The Apostle Paul writes, "Love is patient and kind. Love is not jealous or boastful or proud or rude. Love does not demand its own way." (1 Corinthians 13:4-5b) Without this love, a multiethnic worship team can too easily splinter or drift toward a worship style that reflects only one culture or group.

THE WORSHIP TEAM AND THE CONGREGATION

Members of a multiethnic praise team have the added responsibility of addressing the concerns of a diverse body. The team must be sensitive to cultural norms and different styles of worship. This is not about political correctness, but about seeking authentic unity before God. Leading a multiethnic church or fellowship with music that comes predominately from a single tradition will alienate many worshipers. These individuals may find themselves unsatisfied or uncomfortable, and after a while, they may simply stop attending. Because the makeup of the worship team is varied, each member will bring different ideas and songs—or at least different ways of singing the same songs—to the table. Navigating these differences is never easy, but this hard work is a crucial step in the process of building a sound that the congregation can begin to process and support over time.

This support is critical to the success of multiethnic worship. If the congregation cannot identify with the praise team's vision, it will never embrace the cultural sacrifices required to forge a new multiethnic unity. For this reason, the worship team should do more than suddenly begin playing new songs from varied traditions. Someone must explain to the congregation what is happening, and why the team is making the decisions it makes. Ask your congregation for feedback and support, and invite worshipers to join you in praying for unity and the fulfillment of God's diverse body on earth. Introduce new team members, and discuss the style and history of new songs. Above all, ask God to make the congregation and the worship team of one mind in the pursuit of his full body.

It may be particularly helpful to take inventory of the various traditions represented within the congregation or fellowship at large. Making a commitment to songs and rhythms reflective of these traditions can be an important show of good faith in a diverse group, especially as you begin your transition to multiethnic worship. It also affords the congregation an active role in determining how best to move forward. In majority churches, it is not enough to pay token tribute to minority cultures by including one gospel or foreign language song in a worship set. Members of the music team should seek to understand the significance of these songs within the traditions from which they arise. They must also be able to explain the value of music that crosses cultural boundaries to congregation members and challenge them to move out of comfort zones and open their hearts to the different ways in which God wants to move them.

Here, the special and dynamic relationship between the praise team and the congregation is central. Most congregations are like mirrors—they experience uncertainty when entering initially into worship and look to the praise team for direction. If the praise team projects reticence, the congregation will usually hesitate; if it projects freedom, the congregation will often relax. This makes strong technical preparation an essential part of successful multiethnic worship, especially when the praise team is introducing songs from new traditions with which the congregation may be uncomfortable or stylistically unfamiliar.

Attention to the technical side of worship (the practice and preparation that occurs before leading a group in worship) frees the praise team to worship openly before the congregation. Not having to focus on which harmony to sing, how to transition from one part of a song to another, or what an instrument should be doing at any given point permits the worship team to experience the power that moves through the words and melodies they sing. As the congregation witnesses this display of freedom, it will engage its own capacity to enter into worship without fear or self-conscious anxiety.

Technical preparation also gives team members flexibility in performing each song. By knowing how a song transitions from one part to the next, the worship leader can easily repeat a section or change the order within the song for as long as he or she feels the Spirit moving. The musicians and singers, having been well prepared, need only follow the leader's direction and seamlessly transition with him or her. When the praise team is on the same page musically and spiritually, the result is a climate of freedom. But when the team is not together, the congregation often pays more attention to the uncertain scene in front of them than to the God who dwells in the praises of His people (Psalm 22:3).

What happens in front of the congregation must also be an emotional and spiritual outgrowth of what happens every week during rehearsal. In the midst of practicing and fine-tuning, it is important to make sure that the Spirit is ministering to each member of the worship team. Leading worship should be a privilege, not a chore, and members should make time during rehearsals to praise God without restrictions. If the team has a favorite or particularly motivational set of songs, sing them together, perhaps even a cappella. Have occasional meetings that do not focus on an upcoming service, but rather on rejuvenating the team. Use this time to learn about one another's backgrounds and racial and cultural experiences. Devote particular time to allowing members to share grievances and be candid about any struggles or divisions within the team. Pray together and ask God to overcome these problems by drawing team members together as a unit. When all else fails, submit to one another, and recommit to the shared vision of an authentic, multiethnic worship community.

The process of group cohesion is slow and often challenging, but worship team members should remember that they are building an example for others to follow. Multiethnic fellowship is messy and hard. As a church reevaluates old traditions and inaugurates new ones, it is natural to experience growing pains. Many congregants will wonder how best to adjust to new musical practices that may make them uncomfortable or uncertain. Amid the stress of these changes, a humble but determined praise team can reassure worshipers that transitional discomfort is an integral part of their worship, and that God is big enough to see them through as he builds his body into something more reflective of himself.

13

THE DEMON CALLED RACISM

SUE HAHN GUTIERREZ

What is racism? To describe "racism" as a socio-political construct designed to oppress entire people groups does not give the power of racism its full due. I believe racism is a demonic force that separates us from God and creates division among human beings by "naming" people, giving them a false identity, and creating and maintaining a system of injustice and oppression.

BEING UN-NAMED

One of the hardest intellectual dilemmas that I have grappled with is the nature of race. I believe "race," as it is currently defined, is a socio-political construct that has no true biological or scientific basis. What does it mean to be a part of the "Asian" racial group? Does it comprise people descended from ethnic groups originating in East Asia? What about Southeast Asia? Or South Asia? What do I, as second generation Korean American born in New Jersey, have in common with people from India or Japan or Samoa? Any physical similarities are superficial, inconsistent, and biologically insignificant. Culturally speaking, there may be some similarities but more in the way of differences. Yet I am firmly linked with people from a myriad of ethnic backgrounds in the US Census and in the minds of others. And, to be honest, in my own mind, even though I know full well that it is a false identity and that "Asian" does not make sense as a racial category.

During my years at Amherst College I followed in the footsteps of generations of college students before me, embarking on a quest for my independence and my identity—questioning my assumptions about the world and seeking an answer to the perennial question, "Who am I?" More often than not, I lacked the wisdom to survive this journey unscathed. A large part of that wisdom comes from knowing, believing, and internalizing the identity that one has as a child of God. For most of my life, however, it was not my identity in Christ that defined and drove me but rather, the identity that racism gave me.

Because of racism, we no longer see each other the way that God sees us. Instead, we end up with labels — false identities aimed at creating destructive divisions between people. Racism named me "foreign," "smart," "good-at-math," "exotic," and "submissive," among other things. Most of us believe these false identities despite our best judgment, and these identities end up dividing us on the basis of race. While race may not be a real biological or scientific construct, racism exists and the negative effects that it has on people and society are very real. Indeed, much of my experience as an Asian American Christian has been one of alienation—from people of other races, from other Asian American Christians, from the church, and even from God.

DIVIDED BY FALSE NAMES

One of the ways in which racism divides and alienates people from each other is by naming specific people as oppressors and others as victims, thereby pitting them against each other. For example, people have openly challenged my identity as a minority and the racism that I have experienced. Because I am Asian American rather than black, Latina, or Native American, white people and other minorities have not taken me seriously as someone who has experienced the effects of racism. One girl in high school said to an Indian American friend of ours, "You're not a minority. Your dad's a doctor!" Several years ago, a couple of colleagues challenged me, "You went to Harvard. You have a good career. How can you tell me that you have experienced racial discrimination?"

Racism, however, does not always manifest itself in individual acts of discrimination and prejudice, and the negative consequences of racism are not solely indexed to one's income. Yet the widespread perception that this is what racism looks like means that many people (both Asian Americans and non-Asian Americans) do not legitimize the experiences and identities of Asian Americans as victims of racism and oppression. As an Asian American at Amherst College I was marginalized by both white people and by other people of color, an experience epitomized by three particular incidents.

On April 29, 1992, a Los Angeles jury failed to convict four officers charged with using excessive force to arrest Rodney King. In Los Angeles and in cities elsewhere around the country, the decision resulted in widespread riots and protests. At Amherst College, they resulted in a silent protest led by the Black Students Union (BSU). Overnight, black-dressed effigies suddenly appeared around campus, hung from trees or sprawled on the ground, representing African Americans who had been lynched with impunity in the United States not so long ago. Placards were pinned to bodies, identifying the names of the lynching victims, how they had been killed, and what justice (if any), their murderers faced. Some students did not seem to grasp or did not respect the symbolism and the intent of the protest. Some reportedly began to use the effigies as pillows when they were studying outside on the quad.

The protest organizers did not feel that either the student body or the school administration was sympathetic to their cause, so they staged a takeover of Converse Hall, the college's main administration building. In the middle of the night, a group of students barricaded themselves in the building and issued a letter with a list of demands – hire more faculty of

color, admit more students of color, and institute an ethnic studies program. While I and other Asian Americans supported the demands in principle, we were absolutely livid because the protestors claimed that they
spoke on behalf of all minority students on campus without bothering to
consult with the Asian American community before taking over the building and sending out a list of demands that was supposed to reflect our
goals.

Stereotypically, Asian Americans tend not to be prone to public out-
bursts of anger, but a low-level fury and sense of righteous indignation was
in the air at a hastily-called meeting of the Asian Students Association to
discuss our response to the protesters' actions. After much venting about
our exclusion from the process, heated debate over whether or not to
support the protesters, and some hurried discussions with members of
the Black Student Union, we decided to throw our support behind our
black sisters and brothers with the understanding that if we supported
their current agenda, they would reciprocate in the future and support
us in our own efforts. Future interactions between Asian Americans and
other minority groups on campus, however, continued to be colored by
the perception that Asian Americans were not taken seriously as a minority
group, and this discouraged close relationships across racial lines.

Christians do no better than non-Christians when it comes to legiti-
mizing the identity of Asian Americans as a minority group. In 1994, the
Amherst Christian Fellowship organized a weekend conference on racial
reconciliation with Spencer Perkins and Chris Rice as the featured speakers. I was not involved in organizing the event and remember only being
peripherally involved even in attending the conference.

Chris and Spencer's narrative and the framework they brought to the
table were entirely based on a white-black perspective. They freely ac-
knowledged this upfront, as they were living out racial reconciliation in

an almost exclusively black-white setting in Mississippi. On a purely intellectual level, I fully accepted this and was fine with it–there are not many Asian Americans in Mississippi. But on a gut emotional level, I could not help but roll my eyes and think, "Hey, the world is made up of more than just black and white people!" While I recognized and supported the good intentions of the Fellowship and was pleased that some Christians were trying to tackle this issue, I also proceeded with a distinct lack of enthusiasm, fairly certain that the event would not really be relevant to me.

Ultimately, I was not able to keep my mouth shut and engaged in an exchange with Perkins and Rice about how their model for racial reconciliation applied to people who were not black or white. Chris or Spencer speculated that the situation is different for Asian Americans – that maybe it is not so bad for us – because stereotypes of Asian Americans are positive while stereotypes for African Americans are negative. I do not remember exactly what I said in response, but I remember being annoyed with that observation and challenging them. One of the two told me years later that I had talked about the model minority myth during that discussion. It was the first time they had ever heard the term.

As much as I resent it when people of other races exclude Asian Americans from the table when it comes to fighting racism and delegitimize them as a minority, I know that a part of the problem is that many Asian Americans do not want to be viewed as victims of racism or people of color. The Asian American community frequently chooses to be silent over these issues and deliberately excludes itself from the conversation even though it is not in our best interest to do so. I have found Asian American Christians more passive and silent on issues of racism than non-Christians. Very few Asian American Christians belonged to the Amherst College Asian Students Association or other organizations working to address racism and discrimination.

One of the organizations listed as a co-sponsor of the 1994 racial reconciliation workshop was a local Asian American campus church. In addition to Sunday services, the church had its own Bible Study and fellowship
time on Friday nights. Rice and Perkins' major address was scheduled for
Friday evening. Although the Church had agreed to co-sponsor the event,
its leadership chose to continue to hold its regular Friday night Bible Study
and asked the congregants to come to the Bible Study and skip the Rice
and Perkins event on Friday night, noting that they could still go to the
Saturday events. I was surprised and angered by this announcement – in
my mind, it confirmed yet again my opinion that Asian American Christians were not interested in engaging the greater world on matters of racial
injustice that occur on an on-going basis.

Looking back on these three incidents, I can see in microcosm the greater schisms that occur in society because of racism. Being "Asian American"
was the primary identity that I carried with me over the years, rather than
"follower of Christ." As a result, I have often felt more kinship with other
Asian Americans and the shared experience we endure in the U.S., rather
than with people of other races or ethnicities, even when they are Christians. I suspect this sentiment is not uncommon, and many Asian American
Christians, like many other Christians of color, find it difficult or uncomfortable being part of churches and other institutions that are not predominantly made up people from their own racial group.

THE DEMON CALLED RACISM

I spent a long time trying to make sense of the organized, conspirato-
rial way in which racism oppresses entire people groups and protects the
power and privileges of white people. For example, according to the "middleman minority" theory (Bonacich 1973), the people group that holds the
power in a society makes use of an oppressed minority group as a buffer
zone, a middle man, between themselves and the most-oppressed mem-

bers of society. Rather than owning businesses and providing services that bring them in direct contact with the most-oppressed group, the majority encourages other minority groups to own those business and provide those services so that if the most-oppressed group were to rise up in anger against their oppression, they would take it out on the other minority group rather than the majority group. According to this theory, in the US, it is the Korean dry cleaners and green grocers, Indian gas station owners, and Ethiopian convenience store owners who buffer white people from poor African Americans.

Another, more widely-known theory of Asian American oppression is the "model minority myth" (see, for example, Chin 2001). According to this theory, white people have made Asian Americans complacent in their oppression and pitted them against other minority groups by perpetuating positive stereotypes of Asians and encouraging Asian Americans to believe in the assertion that American society is a meritocracy where society equally rewards all those willing to work hard and follow "the system." In the early years of Asian immigration to the US in the nineteenth and early twentieth centuries, stereotypes of Asians were quite negative – we were sneaky, unreliable, cunning, out to steal American jobs, never to be seen as "real" Americans but rather, perpetually foreign. After the Civil Rights movement, there was a shift in stereotypes, and though we were still foreign, we also became smart, hard-working, and good in math, with a strong, laudable commitment to family, education, and community. We were living proof that if you worked hard and played by the rules, you would get ahead and the meritocracy would work for you. Implicitly, and sometimes explicitly, Asian Americans were held up in contrast to other minorities, a reproof that they ought to stop causing trouble and challenging the existing power structure and that if they just behaved like us, they too would get ahead.

It was difficult for me to accept either the middleman minority theory or model minority myth because I could not accept that there was a conspiracy of white people smart enough, powerful enough, and organized enough to come up with two such effective strategies for not only oppressing people of color but also playing divide-and-conquer so that we did not unite against them. However, I have seen and experienced the effects of both these strategies in powerful ways that I cannot deny.

When asked to describe what characterizes Asians as a racial group, many Asian Americans will indeed repeat back the prevailing stereotype (hard-working, family-oriented, placing a high value on education) even though there are plenty of lazy and uneducated Asian Americans. Many Asians in Asia and many Asian Americans do not even think of themselves as "Asian" or part of a single racial group, but rather as Korean, Taiwanese, Filipino, Lao, or Karen. Many Asian Americans have also chosen to believe in an American meritocracy. Because a significant number of Asian Americans have found some level of economic success and security, we do not believe that racism has impacted us in a negative way. Even if we do observe racism and discrimination directed against us, many Asian Americans are unwilling to challenge the status quo. One has only to look at the aftermath of the Rodney King verdict and the LA riots to see the fruit of the Middleman Minority strategy. Though it was a group of white police officers who beat Rodney King and a white-dominated judicial system that acquitted the white police officers, it was the Korean-owned small businesses located in their neighborhoods that African Americans destroyed in their protests and rioting.

It has only been within the last few years, as a member of my church's racial justice ministry, that I have been able to reconcile my unwillingness to believe that racism is an intentionally-organized system of oppression with the very real evidence that racism is indeed very organized and very effective. Revelation, for me, finally came through the scriptures.

Jesus tells us in John 10:1-10 that Satan has come to kill, steal, and destroy. One of the ways in which Satan does this is through the world's systems, institutions, and power structures. The scripture states that "our struggle is not against flesh and blood, but against the rulers, against the authorities, against the powers of this dark world and against the spiritual forces of evil in the heavenly realms." (Ephesians 6:12). Colossians 2:8 further warns us, "See to it that no one takes you captive through hollow and deceptive philosophy, which depends on human tradition and the basic principles of this world rather than on Christ."

Satan uses racism to make the systems, institutions, and power structures in which we live unjust—making them structures in which some people have a disproportionate amount of power and privilege and in which other people are oppressed and divided against each other. It is spiritual warfare waged through political, economic, social, and sometimes military means. As I began to view racism through the lens of spiritual warfare, I began to accept that it is indeed a conspiracy, a conspiracy breathed by a demonic force and maintained through human frailty, rather than one solely conceived by human minds. This system creates false identities and distorts our understanding of each other, so that we no longer see each other the way that God sees us. These untruths and distortions divide the people of God and allow us to perpetrate injustices on both an individual basis (e.g., believing a racial stereotype or committing an act of discrimination) and on a systemic basis (e.g., creating school systems that provide fewer resources to schools predominantly made up of minority students). These untruths and distortions also have a devastating effect on the Church.

When people think of racism and the Church, they tend to think of the big things, like the failure of many white churches to support the Civil Rights movement. Racism, however, often works in more subtle ways to undermine churches. My church calls itself a multi-denominational, evangelical church, and its vision is to become a living embodiment of God's call to be one people across denominations, class, race, political affiliation, and other differences that tend to divide Christians. It is a difficult vision to fulfill, and this church has endured some very painful struggles and a major congregational rift because of racism.

When this church was founded it was a predominantly white congregation located in a poor, predominantly African American section of Washington, DC. In an effort to become a multi-racial congregation that also addressed the needs of the surrounding neighborhood, the church did many of the things that other churches do in an effort to attract more people of color. It hired a black pastor to lead the congregation and incorporated more African American styles of worship. The church has also, at various times, housed a methadone clinic, a school for low-income students, and before and after-care programs for children in the neighborhood. Individual members strive to do justly, love mercy, and walk humbly with God on a daily basis (Micah 6:8) in such myriad ways as attending worship services that protest genocide in the Sudan, supporting local agriculture that practices good environmental and labor practices, and buying new glasses for a poor, elderly African American gentleman who came to know Christ through this church and buys candy every Sunday for the children of the church even though he has very little money for his own needs.

Despite these efforts, this church has never been able to become a truly multi-racial congregation. This is not just because the neighborhood rapidly gentrified into a white, upper middle class community. The congregation has remained predominantly white because many of the efforts made to attract and keep people of color have mostly to do with changing surface features of the church like worship style without addressing the underlying problems caused by racism. One of the biggest problems faced by this church was the unwillingness of white congregants and leaders to give up the power and authority necessary to transform the church. This was not intentional racial discrimination but rather the inability of those people who were already in power (who are white) to see how the existing church culture, power structure, policies, and practices are related to race and result in the maintenance their own power, preferences, and privileges.

Though the church called a black man to serve as the senior pastor in order move towards its vision of becoming a multi-racial church, white congregants ended up feeling threatened both by the changes the African American pastor attempted to bring to the church and by his style of leadership. When trying to implement initiatives aimed at making people of color feel more welcome at the church, incorporating different worship styles, preaching sermons on racism, or raising the profile of church ministries focusing on the needs of the neighborhood, the pastor and other church members were seen as neglecting the needs and priorities of other (white) members of the church. Raised in a Pentecostal, black church, the pastor was used to a leadership model where the senior pastor exercised a great deal of authority over the congregation, including lay leaders. Our congregation, however, was used to a church leadership model where the senior pastor was just one of many leaders and did not exercise special authority. Though the pastor was nowhere close to being authoritarian, some congregants reacted very negatively to his leadership style. While members of the church were not maliciously and intentionally exercising racial discrimination, I saw how racism, as a spiritual force, caused conflict and division in the church body along racial lines.

FINDING MY NAME

My current walk with God is markedly different from the way in which I lived out my faith for most of my life. The turning point was graduate school. Before graduate school, my spiritual life was inconsistent at best, punctuated by occasional bursts of spiritual fervor when I would feel a real emotional connection to God and commit to become a better Christian by praying harder, reading the Bible more, and getting more involved with church or the Amherst Christian Fellowship. These moments were short-lived, and I never sustained those commitments. I would inevitably slide back into a life of irregular church attendance and even less regular practice of the basic Christian disciplines. And outside of those burst of spiritual fervor, I never felt particularly close to God.

I was also unable to find a church where I felt I belonged. Though I felt a strong sense of connection with my Asian American friends, I never truly felt that I belonged to a predominantly Asian American church. For as long as I can remember, I have had a passion for social and economic justice and particularly for racial reconciliation. None of the Asian American churches I attended did much to explicitly nurture a commitment to social or racial justice as part of Christian discipleship, and this omission made me feel as much as an outsider in Asian American churches as I did in predominantly white churches.

During my first semester of public policy graduate school, I slid swiftly and easily into old habits when it came to practicing the Christian disciplines—I did not attend church regularly, and I was not a particularly committed member of the Christian Fellowship. That eventually changed, however, as I began to learn for the first time that God cares deeply about justice — justice of the social/economic/political/racial sort and not just justice as it pertains to sin, morality, and personal righteousness before God.

The graduate school InterVarsity Christian Fellowship (IVCF) helped me and many other students think about how to live out our Christian faith in two very important ways. First, we were encouraged to integrate our faith and public life as politicians, policy-makers, and public leaders; second, we were challenged to live lives that are radically committed to justice. I also began attending a church with a congregation that had a heart for the poor and the oppressed. Though I did not enjoy the worship style as much as that at other churches, I loved this church more than any other church I had attended because of the congregation's commitment to Christian community and to justice issues.

While my current church still struggles with its mission of becoming a multi-racial and multi-cultural community and is still a predominantly white church in terms of demographics and culture, it is a place that has helped me to grow in my faith because it is a place that has encouraged and helped me in understanding my true identity — both as a child of God and as a person of color. While the church has failed to achieve its ideals and has allowed racism to create division within the community, it has also done more than any other church I have attended in attempting to address the systematic and individual injustices resulting from racism. God is more real to me now than He had ever been before, and He is a daily presence now in a way that was not true in the past. In Isaiah 58:6-8, God tells us that worship and justice are inextricably linked together, and I believe that as I become more obedient to God's commands concerning justice, I become more of a true worshiper of God.

14

CONCLUSION

PAUL SORRENTINO

In the introduction of Part I we invited you to join us on a continuing journey. Now it is time to thank you for coming along and to renew the invitation. I suspect that divisions among people, for all sorts of reasons, will continue until Christ's return. The Church is called to be a healer and peacemaker in overcoming those divides and to bring justice and righteousness to bear in people's lives and circumstances. Below, I highlight some of the key lessons that we have learned in the racial reconciliation and multiethnic journey. Some of these may come easy for you as an individual, your church or fellowship. Others may be long-term projects that are a real challenge. We think all of them are worth pursuing.

A KEY LEADER OR LEADERS in the church need to be committed to multiethnic ministry. Bill Hybels, of Willow Creek Community Church, has made such a commitment in recent years. In a meeting with church leaders from around the country, he stated:

> In every congregation, someone has to have a vision for what the church should be biblically and then the practicality to ask, "How do we move toward that?" In my opinion, a church doesn't have much of a chance of [becoming multicultural] until the senior pastor has a "conversion experience" about this issue (Gilbreath 2006, 172)

The reason for this is that a commitment to becoming multiethnic involves many choices. Who will guest speakers be? Will the list include people of color? What illustrations will be used in sermons? Who will be in key leadership roles and in visible leadership positions? All of these are decisions that may well have push-back from leaders and members of the congregation. It will take someone with respect and authority as well as commitment to make the changes that will be needed to create a culture of unity in Christ across difference.

CONGREGATIONAL BUY-IN is essential. This will, understandably, take the longest time. It means that the church's commitment to multiethnicity needs to be clear and before the people. Emerson's research on successful multi-racial churches showed the value of a written statement in helping the church to shape priorities appropriately. He describes the results in the case of Wilcrest Baptist Church in Houston:

> With the creation of the vision statement came strategic changes in an effort to conform to its meaning. These changes included over a decade of changing the music (the changes continue) and diversifying the leadership (this too, continually evolves). Many efforts were made to connect to the surrounding community, including marches, visits to homes, hosting festivals, movie nights, and creating programs for parents of young children, for teens, and for non-native English speakers, to name a few." (Emerson and Woo 2006, 72)

During most of the time that I was working with the Amherst Christian Fellowship, our purpose statement read: "In response to God's love, grace and truth: The purpose of the Amherst Christian Fellowship is to establish and advance a witnessing community of students, staff, administrators and faculty who follow Jesus as Savior and Lord: Growing in love for God, God's Word, God's people of every ethnicity and culture, and God's purposes in the world." A good written statement helps us to set priorities and measure progress.

RESPONSIBILITY MUST BE SHARED. The above principles help to set the stage for this one. In general, whites tend to gravitate toward leadership roles. In a multiethnic setting, the common experience is that whites speak up more. Without debating the cause for this, it is important that ethnic minorities be given a voice. In our leadership meetings, we found it helpful to practice what Eric Law calls "mutual-invitation." The leader begins by introducing a conversation and saying something about it. He or she then invites a different person, person X to comment. Person X may say something or chose to pass. In either case, person X invites the next person, person Y, to speak. Person Y then either says something or passes, but person Y then invites the next person and so on until everyone has had the opportunity to make a comment (Law 1993, 113-114). This is a valuable way to affirm and respect each person regardless of to what degree he or she might be an introvert or and extrovert and regardless of his or her cultural mores about speaking in a group.

Shared responsibility includes leadership positions that are vital for decision making as well as visible to the congregation, such as leading worship, up-front prayer, announcements and preaching. Relationships in a multiethnic fellowship may require an added emphasis in taking on the attitude of Christ Jesus:

> *Who, being in very nature God, did not consider equality with God something to be grasped, but made himself nothing, taking the very nature of a servant, being made in human likeness. And being found in appearance as a man, he humbled himself and became obedient to death—even death on a cross!* (Phil. 2:6-8)

This may also require that the congregation be willing to view leadership selection differently. A common short-hand term for leadership selection in some circles is FAT— one looks for those who are Faithful, Available and Teachable. These terms may need to be re-evaluated in light of differing needs of members and the expectations and assumptions behind these terms examined. A person with multiple and essential roles outside of church may not appear faithful or available by some measurements when, in reality, he or she is being obedient to Christ in caring for and providing for family.

MULTIETHNICITY IS NOT AN END IN ITSELF. We are not making a call to political correctness in this book. Being a multiethnic congregation is part of what it means to be a fully functioning Christian body with differing parts. It is what it means to fulfill Jesus' prayer that we "may be one... so that the world may believe that you have sent me...May they be brought to complete unity to let the world know that you sent me and have loved them even as you have loved me" (John 17:21, 23). Multiethnic congregations speak to the watching world of the love of God in an especially powerful way. This was the experience Chris and Jon described in Section I. What they observed in the lives and practice of a multiethnic fellowship drew them to faith in Christ. Bill Hybels, once again, addresses this issue:

> Willow Creek started in the era when the church-growth people were saying, "Don't dissipate any of your energies fighting race issues. Focus everything on evangelism." It was the homogeneous-unit principle of church growth. And I remember as a young pastor thinking, "That's true." I didn't know whether I wanted to chance alienating people who were seekers, whose eternity was on the line, and who might only come to church one time. I wanted to take away as many obstacles as possible, other than the cross, to help people focus on the gospel. So now, thirty years later...I recognize that a true biblically functioning community must include being multiethnic (Gilbreath 2006, 170-171).

Our unity in Christ should serve to strengthen the fellowship's outward focus and commitment to accomplishing God's purposes in the world.

HEALTHY RELATIONSHIPS are at the heart of a multiethnic fellowship. This will take extra work outside of a Sunday morning service. We need to take time to learn about each other, to listen to each other's stories about our upbringing, family background and life circumstances. It means learning about what is important to each other. People of color spend a great deal of time in majority white culture. This is generally not true of whites in minority culture. Whites have a special responsibility to go to events that are significant to people of color, especially those in your congregation, to meet family members, to read books and see movies that are popular with ethnic groups outside one's own. It means learning about differing political perspectives and listening to why they are held as well as learning about and appreciating different styles of worship and theological approaches. Clearly, these things will not happen easily or automatically.

INTENTIONALITY IS VITAL if the things mentioned above are to happen. This journey takes a detour from the interstate highway system. It means a change in priorities and the status quo of how things are done in the fellowship as well as outside of the formal fellowship activities. It means becoming real friends. I like the way the Apostle Paul said it in 1 Thessalonians 2:8: "We loved you so much that we were delighted to share with you not only the gospel of God but our lives as well, because you had become so dear to us." That is the nature of relationships we are called to have.

FAITH IN ACTION is what Jesus has called us to. He even said that our relationship with the Trinity would be deepened when we obey his commands: "Whoever has my commands and obeys them, he is the one who loves me. He who loves me will be loved by my Father, and I too will love him and show myself to him" (John 14:21). Faith in action is what Rick Warren meant when he said we now need a second reformation. The first reformation was about creeds, what we believe, but the second reformation is about deeds, what we do (Boorstein Feb. 5, 2008). Both are important. Working side-by-side in our efforts to build a just society is a powerful way to build relationships across ethnic lines and to live out our faith before the watching world.

AUTHENTICITY or genuineness is a key quality in both cross-ethnic relations and relations with youth. This generation of young people in their teens and twenties has been referred to as "crap detectors." They seem especially alert to when someone is putting on a show and being inauthentic. This same principle is true for ethnic minorities in their interactions with majority people. It is especially vital for leaders to prove themselves trustworthy, to follow through on their commitments and to be conscious of living out their faith.

It is also worth commenting on the youthfulness of many of the contributing authors of this book. People in their twenties and teens have grown up in a society that values multiculturalism. They are used to diverse classroom settings and sports teams. It is what they expect. When they do not see it in the church they are disillusioned. For the sake of the gospel and for the future of the church, we need to make multiethnic congregations a priority. It is the way of Jesus.

A LONG JOURNEY: We also need to encourage one another to persist, even when progress seems elusive. As the apostle Paul wrote to the Galatians:

> Let us not become weary in doing good, for at the proper time we will reap a harvest if we do not give up. Therefore, as we have opportunity, let us do good to all people, especially to those who belong to the family of believers (Gal. 6:9-10).

We invite you to continue this journey toward multiethnic fellowship with us. We have not pretended that it is easy, but I hope we have expressed clearly that it is worth it. One of the most popular hymns in many churches was written by a slave ship captain who later was converted to Christianity and became an Anglican priest and abolitionist, John Newton (1725-1807). The first stanza of his hymn, Amazing Grace, is a fitting way to conclude A Transforming Vision. We invite you to affirm your commitment to continue with us in this journey of transformation. We pray that you will.

> Amazing Grace, how sweet the sound,
>
> That saved a wretch like me.
>
> I once was lost but now am found,
>
> Was blind, but now I see.

Appendix 1

Biblical Foundations for multiethnic Fellowship

Paul Sorrentino

The greatest ethnic divide in the Bible is between Jews and Gentiles, that is, all people who are not Jewish. A second great divide is between rich and poor. More than 1,200 scripture passages talk about God's concern for the poor and oppressed, and our responsibility to do right by them (Perry 2002, 55). The Bible teaches that our love should go beyond personal relationships to also address real pain and harm that may come upon others. These two biblical themes — reconciliation across ethnic barriers, and justice for the poor — come together to establish the foundation for Christian thinking about race and ethnicity in the church. What follows is a survey of those biblical foundations, from Genesis to Revelation, beginning with the theme of Reconciliation.

FOUNDATIONS FOR RECONCILIATION IN THE HEBREW SCRIPTURES

Creation. God created the world and called it "very good" (Gen. 1:31). God created humankind in his image (Gen. 1:27-28) and thus gave every person worth and dignity as his image bearers. It is our common ancestry. The value of humankind is underscored by Christ taking on human form in the incarnation and by his death and resurrection to bring restoration to a broken humanity.

Noah and God's covenant with all creation. God judged humankind in the Genesis flood because "every inclination of the thoughts of his heart was only evil all the time" (Gen. 6:5). Noah and his family, however, were protected because "Noah was a righteous man, blameless among the people of his time, and he walked with God" (Gen. 6:9). After the flood, God made a covenant with Noah (Gen.

9:1-17). Covenants were common place in ancient times and they reflected the highest level of commitment and promise between two parties. Williamson writes that "the universal scope of this covenant implies that the blessing for which humanity was created and the creation that had been preserved through the flood will ultimately encompass not just one people or nation, but rather the whole earth" (Williamson 2003, 141).

Babel. Two chapters later, the Bible records that there was only one language and that people wanted to remain together in one place. They were resisting God's intent that people spread out and fill the earth (Gen. 1:28). So God intervened at Babel in order to confuse their language and bring about his plan that humankind be scattered over the earth (Gen. 11:1-9). This dispersion enabled the development of differing cultures, ethnicities and languages

Abraham and God's blessing for all peoples. Although people were now scattered, this did not diminish God's concern for all of humankind. The next chapter in the Bible tells of God's call to Abram, who would later be renamed Abraham. At the time, Abram was living in Haran, located in modern day Turkey.

The LORD had said to Abram:

Leave your country, your people and your father's household and go to the land I will show you. "I will make you into a great nation and I will bless you; I will make your name great, and you will be a blessing.

I will bless those who bless you, and whoever curses you I will curse; and all peoples on earth will be blessed through you" (Gen. 12:1-3).

In this covenant with the first patriarch of Israel, God promised to bless "all peoples on earth" through Abraham.[1] This remarkable covenant of blessing to all people was renewed with Abraham's descendants, Isaac (Gen. 26:4) and Jacob (Gen. 28:13-15).

Moses. Moses was born to a Hebrew family while the Israelites were slaves in Egypt. As an infant, he was rescued from the Nile River by Pharaoh's daughter and raised in the royal household. After he murdered an Egyptian, in defense of a Hebrew slave, Moses fled to the wilderness of Midian, east of the Red Sea. There he worked as a shepherd for forty years until God spoke to him from the burning bush. He then returned to Egypt, in obedience to God's command (Exod. 3:7-10), and led the Israelites out of Egypt (Exod. 4:18-

---

1 See also Gen. 15:1-21; 17:1-8; 18:17-19 and 22:17-18.

14:31). Moses married a dark skinned Cushite woman (from ancient Ethiopia, south of Egypt) and her ethnicity became a source of indignation for Moses' brother and sister (Num. 12:1-2). Israel's great leader lived in three different cultures, was educated in Pharaoh's palace and worked in the wilderness as a shepherd, and he married outside of his ethnic, and probably racial, group.

The Prophets and the light to the gentiles. Throughout the Old Testament, God repeatedly affirms his commitment to the welfare and salvation of all people (e.g. Pss. 67:1,7; 96; 100; 105; Prov. 8:15-31; Isa. 45:22; 52:10; Joel 2:28-32). While the Bible does speak about judgment and war, God's broader and ultimate focus is that all people would come to him. In Isaiah 49:6, God said,

> It is too small a thing for you to be my servant to restore the tribes of Jacob and bring back those of Israel I have kept. I will also make you a light for the Gentiles, that you may bring my salvation to the ends of the earth.

Jonah and the renewal of Israel's mission. The prophet Jonah struggled with his own prejudice when God commanded him to go to Nineveh and warn the people of their pending judgment if they did not repent. Nineveh was an Assyrian city near present day Mosul in Iraq. The Assyrians were long standing enemies of the Israelites. Jonah disobeyed God by instead going by ship in the opposite direction from Nineveh. After three days in the belly of a large fish, he finally repented and was disgorged by the fish onto shore. Jonah then obeyed God and went to warn the people of Nineveh. When they repented, Jonah was angry and disconsolate. The book concludes with God's admonition to Jonah (Jon. 4:11): "Nineveh has more than a hundred and twenty thousand people who cannot tell their right hand from their left, and many cattle as well. Should I not be concerned about that great city?" God cared about the Ninevites, even when his prophet did not. God's concern has always been for all people of every ethnicity and culture.

FOUNDATIONS FOR RECONCILIATION IN THE NEW TESTAMENT

The nations in Matthew's Gospel. The Gospel of Matthew was likely written shortly after the destruction of the Jerusalem temple in 70 A.D. It was a time when Jewish-Gentile relations were especially acrimonious. As noted earlier, the greatest divide in the Bible, and especially the New Testament, is between Jew and Gentile. Matthew begins with a genealogy of Jesus (Matt. 1:1-17). Although it was not a requirement to list women in genealogies, Matthew lists four. More significantly, none of the four are the Jewish matriarchs that might be expected: Sarah, Rebekah, Leah, or Rachel. Instead, he records four Gentile women: Tamar (Gen. 38:1-26); Rahab (Josh. 2:1); Ruth (Ruth 1:4) and Bathsheba, whose ethnicity is not certain, but she was married to a Hittite named Uriah [2 Sam. 11:3] (Keener 1993, 46). Matthew chose to emphasize the Gentile and Jewish aspects of Jesus' lineage. Craig Keener, a New Testament scholar, comments,

> When Matthew cites these four women, he is reminding his readers that three ancestors of King David and the mother of King Solomon were Gentiles. Matthew thus declares that the Gentiles were never an afterthought in God's plan but had been part of his work in history from the beginning. This point fits an emphasis that runs throughout Matthew's Gospel (for example 2:1; 3:9; 4:15; 8:11; 28:19), that God is not only for people from our own race or culture; we must cross racial and cultural boundaries to evangelize the whole world, humbly learn from other cultures, and serve with our brothers and sisters there. (Keener 1997, 55)

Matthew goes on to use other examples of key Gentiles. Magi came from the east and gave proper homage to the "king of the Jews" (Matt. 2:2). Jesus was referring to a Roman officer when he said, "I tell you the truth, I have not found anyone in Israel with such great faith" (Matt. 8:10). Similarly, Jesus healed a Canaanite woman and said to her, "Woman, you have great faith" (Matt. 15:28). The Gospel of Matthew concludes with Jesus' command for his followers to "go and make disciples of all the nations" [Matt. 28:19](Keener 1996).

Luke, Jesus and the gentiles. The Gospel of Luke records an important incident when Jesus was in his hometown synagogue in Nazareth. He stood to read and the scroll handed to him was Isaiah. The passage Jesus read was Isaiah 61:1-2.

> "The Spirit of the Lord is on me, because he has anointed me to preach good news to the poor. He has sent me to proclaim freedom for the prisoners and recovery of sight for the blind, to release the oppressed, to proclaim the year of the Lord's favor" (Luke 4:18-19)

Jesus then said, "this scripture is fulfilled in your hearing" (Luke 4:21). He went on to say that a prophet is not honored in his hometown and used two examples to illustrate his point. He told about when Elijah and Elisha each performed miracles with Gentiles outside of Israel (Luke 4:23-27; see also 1 Kings 17:8ff; 2 Kings 5:1ff). It was after Jesus told the Elijah and Elisha stories that the people tried to throw him off a cliff (Luke 4:28-30). Craig Keener says that the main point of these illustrations, and what angered the synagogue members, was "that non-Jews were the ones to accept two of the major signs prophets of the Old Testament. Sidon and Syria were among the particularly despised areas. Jesus' point: Nazareth will not receive him, but non-Jews will" (Keener 1993, 200). Once again, the emphasis is that Jesus' mission was to include all people.

Jesus and the Samaritans. Jesus' most well known parable, the parable of the Good Samaritan, is recorded in Luke 10. A religious leader, an expert in the law, asked Jesus, "What must I do to inherit eternal life?" Rather than respond directly, Jesus asked the questioner what he thought he must do. The man responded by conflating two Old Testament texts in Luke 10:27:

"Love the Lord your God with all your heart and with all your soul and with all your strength and with all your mind" (Deut. 6:5); and, "Love your neighbor as yourself" (Lev. 19:18).

Jesus agreed with the leader's response and told him, "Do this and you will live." It was only after the religious leader wanted more clarification about exactly who his neighbor was, that Jesus told the parable of the Good Samaritan. In the parable, an unidentified man was severely beaten by robbers and left for dead. Interestingly, since he had been stripped of his clothes, his ethnic identity would have been ambiguous. Two different Jewish religious leaders saw him and walked on past him without stopping. However, a Samaritan man had pity, stopped and took care of the man's wounds, and then the Samaritan carried the injured man on his own donkey to an inn where he paid for his care. In this dramatic contrast of responses, Jesus used the Gentile Samaritan to illustrate the principle of loving "your neighbor as yourself." Jesus never explicitly answered the expert in the law's question, "who is my neighbor?" Rather, Jesus used the Samaritan to demonstrate that the fulfillment of the law comes from our own actions of being neighborly and not from our interactions with a specific person or group of people (Luke 10:25-37).

John's Gospel and Jesus call to Unity. The most famous verse in the Bible, John 3:16, says, "For God so loved the world that he gave his one and only Son, that whoever believes in him shall not perish but have eternal life." Once again, God's focus is the whole world. John 4 tells the story of Jesus' crossing a significant ethnic and gender divide through his conversation with a Samaritan woman at a well.

This gentile woman, and many others from the town, became followers of Jesus.

Jesus concluded his "upper room discourse," recorded in John 13-17, with a prayer for his disciples. He prayed for those who were already his disciples and those who would become his followers:

My prayer is not for them alone. I pray also for those who will believe in me through their message, that all of them may be one, Father, just as you are in me and I am in you. May they also be in us so that the world may believe that you have sent me. I have given them the glory that you gave me, that they may be one as we are one: I in them and you in me. May they be brought to complete unity to let the world know that you sent me and have loved them even as you have loved me (John 17:20-23).

His prayer was that his future disciples would have a relationship with one another that reflected the essential oneness of the Father and the Son as members of the Trinity. The nature of the disciples' involvement with one another, across any lines of difference, would speak to the world about the reality of Christ's incarnation and of God's love for the world. "Complete unity" is a high standard. It is only when we are brought to complete unity that the world will understand that the Father sent Jesus into the world and that God loves the world. Conversely, if God's people, the church, are divided, then the rest of the world has little reason to believe in the reality of Christ's coming or God's love. That is a sobering thought. Jesus prayed that we would be filled with the transcending love of God that bridges all divides.

Acts and the mission of the Church. The Acts of the Apostles begins with Jesus' instructions to his disciples that they will be his "witnesses in Jerusalem, and in all Judea and Samaria, and to the ends of the earth" (Acts 1:8). Acts is a testimony to the power of the gospel to cross ethnic, cultural and class separations. Acts itself follows Jesus' directive in Acts 1:8 as the disciples were witnesses first in Jerusalem (Acts 1-7), then in Judea and Samaria (Acts 8-12) and to the ends of the earth (Acts 13-28). The "ends of the earth" for the disciples was functionally the center of the Roman Empire. Acts concludes with the apostle Paul in Rome.

Pentecost and the multiethnic Kingdom. Acts 2 records an extensive list of people from many nations who were present for Peter's Pentecost sermon. The countries represented are grouped in five by John Stott, the British preacher and author. Stott organizes the countries geographically from East to West: 1) the Caspian Sea westward;

2) Asia Minor or present day Turkey; 3) North Africa; 4) Rome; and 5) a combination of Arabs and Cretans (Stott 1990, 63-65). John Stott concludes his comments about Acts 2 this way:

Nothing could have demonstrated more clearly than this the multi-racial, multi-national, multi-lingual nature of the kingdom of Christ. Ever since the early church fathers, commentators have seen the blessing of Pentecost as a deliberate and dramatic reversal of the curse of Babel. At Babel human languages were confused and the nations were scattered; in Jerusalem the language barrier was supernaturally overcome as a sign that the nations would now be gathered together in Christ, prefiguring the great day when the redeemed company will be drawn 'from every nation, tribe, people and language'. Besides, at Babel earth proudly tried to ascend to heaven, whereas in Jerusalem heaven humbly descended to earth (Stott 1990, 68).

Galatians and multiethnic fellowship in the Church. In Galatians, Paul writes of a problem in Antioch with Peter (also called Cephas). Peter had been with the Antiochan believers for several days and had been eating with the Gentiles. When, however, some Jewish believers came from Jerusalem, he stopped that practice and ate only with the Jews. Now Peter was acting as if the Gentiles were second class citizens and were not equal to Jewish believers. Peter's influence was substantial and the other Jewish believers followed his lead, including Barnabas.

Paul did not see this as a minor offense. He saw this as an injustice that threatened the unity of the church. Was salvation in some sense now being made contingent on following the law? As Paul wrote to the Galatians:

Consider Abraham:"He believed God, and it was credited to him as righteousness." Understand, then, that those who believe are children of Abraham. The Scripture foresaw that God would justify the Gentiles by faith, and announced the gospel in advance to Abraham:"All nations will be blessed through you" (Gal. 3:6-8).

Salvation was by faith and not by obedience to the law. Paul publicly challenged Peter for his hypocrisy and modeled the need to actively take a stand against injustice (Gal. 2:11-21).

Ephesians and reconciliation in the Church. In Ephesians 2:13-22, Paul writes about the dividing wall of separation between Jews and Gentiles:

But now in Christ Jesus you who once were far away have been brought near through the blood of Christ. For he himself is our peace, who has made the two one and has destroyed the barrier, the dividing wall of hostility, by abolishing in his flesh the law with its commandments and regulations. His purpose was to create in himself one new man out of the two, thus making peace, and in this one body to reconcile both of them to God through the cross, by which he put to death their hostility. He came and preached peace to you who were far away and peace to those who were near. For through him we both have access to the Father by one Spirit...In him the whole building is joined together and rises to become a holy temple in the Lord. And in him you too are being built together to become a dwelling in which God lives by his Spirit.

In Christ Jesus, the division between Gentiles and Jews was removed. It was not the differences that were problematic, but the barriers that separated them. God's design is that we be united together by his Spirit. God desires to see harmony where there was previously discord. Christ is our head and we are his temple. It is a metaphor that speaks of oneness and difference; of unity and diversity, but not of barriers.

Revelation and the vision of multiethnic worship. The final book in the New Testament is Revelation. The apostle John describes his vision of a group of people worshipping God along with the heavenly hosts. It is a fitting way to conclude this survey of God's desire for all people to worship him together.

After this I looked, and there before me was a great multitude that no one could count, from every nation, tribe, people and language, standing before the throne and in front of the Lamb. They were wearing white robes and were holding palm branches in their hands. And they cried out in a loud voice: "Salvation belongs to our God, who sits on the throne, and to the Lamb" (Rev. 7:9-10).

If we will worship in a multiracial, multinational, multilingual, and multiethnic throng in heaven, it makes sense that we should begin to do it now. If God intends us to worship together for eternity, it must surely be our finest form of praise to God.

THE BIBLICAL CALL TO JUSTICE

Isaiah: Loose the chains of injustice. In Isaiah 58, there is an unambiguous statement of the kind of behavior God expects from people. He wants to see his people address systemic wrongs and to meet the needs of the poor and hungry. If they do that, then God will answer their prayers.

"Is not this the kind of fasting I have chosen: to loose the chains of injustice and untie the cords of the yoke, to set the oppressed free and break every yoke? Is it not to share your food with the hungry and to provide the poor wanderer with shelter—when you see the naked, to clothe him, and not to turn away from your own flesh and blood? Then your light will break forth like the dawn, and your healing will quickly appear; then your righteousness will go before you, and the glory of the LORD will be your rear guard. Then you will call, and the LORD will answer; you will cry for help, and he will say: Here am I" (Isaiah 58:6-9).

Jeremiah: Defend the cause of the poor. Jeremiah was a prophet in Judah for 40 years from King Josiah until the fall of Jerusalem in about 587 BC. Josiah instituted religious reform in a time of extreme corruption and was largely a good king. The kings to follow him were not. Josiah's son, Jehoiakim, became king after him. Under his rule, the nation returned to idolatry and he directly opposed Jeremiah as a prophet of God. God reprimanded Jehoiakim through Jeremiah. In one concise and clear statement, the Lord spoke to Jehoiakim of his father, King Josiah:

"He defended the cause of the poor and needy, and so all went well. Is that not what it means to know me?" declares the LORD (Jer. 22:16)

The Lord's warning to Jehoiakim makes it clear that caring for the poor and needy is a vital expression of our knowing God. It is not a liberal or conservative political value. It is what faithful people do.

Amos: Maintain justice. The prophet Amos called the people to repentance for their mistreatment of the poor and righteous. He admonished the people to "seek good, not evil" and to "maintain justice in the courts." If they did that, then God would be with them (Amos 5:14-15). Rather than hypocritical religious fervor, God's desire was for the people to "let justice roll on like a river, righteousness like a never-failing stream!" (Amos 5:24)

Micah: Act justly. The prophet Micah stated God's desire simply:

He has showed you, O man, what is good. And what does the LORD require of you? To act justly and to love mercy and to walk humbly with your God. (Mic. 6:8)

This single verse provides direction for godly living. There are three criteria for evaluating our conduct: 1) are we acting justly? 2) are we acting mercifully? and 3) are we genuinely humble as we walk in the light of God?

Matthew: I was hungry and you gave me something to eat. In Matthew 25, Jesus describes a scene from the final judgment. All the nations will be gathered before the Son of Man and he will separate people based on their behavior. Using a shepherd analogy, he says that the sheep will go to his right and the goats to his left. Then he went on to say:

Then the King will say to those on his right, 'Come, you who are blessed by my Father; take your inheritance, the kingdom prepared for you since the creation of the world. For I was hungry and you gave me something to eat, I was thirsty and you gave me something to drink, I was a stranger and you invited me in, I needed clothes and you clothed me, I was sick and you looked after me, I was in prison and you came to visit me(Matt. 25:35-36).

As Jesus continues the judgment story, those called "blessed by my Father" ask the Lord, in some confusion, when they had done any of these things for him? The Lord answers them, "I tell you the truth, whatever you did for one of the least of these brothers of mine, you did for me" (Matt. 25:40).

The treatment of the hungry, thirsty, homeless, imprisoned and poor are all bases of demonstrating the reality of our faith. Our treatment of people made in God's image is considered to be treatment of Jesus. Those who did not care for the needs of others did not enter the kingdom (Matt. 25:41-46).

Luke: A warning to the rich. In Luke 16, Jesus tells a parable of a rich man and a poor man. The poor man, Lazarus, died and went to a seat of honor by Abraham in the afterlife. The rich man went to Hades. In his suffering, the wealthy man saw Abraham and Lazarus and cried out to Abraham for help. He was told that he received his good things in life while Lazarus did not. Lazarus, on the other hand, received his rewards in the afterlife. After the rich man's request was refused, he asked for a warning to be sent to his five brothers. He was told that their only warning, and an adequate one at that, was what they already knew from Moses and the Prophets (Luke 16:19-31). In this passage, Jesus makes the point that how we use wealth in the care of others is a factor in our eternal standing before God.

Galatians: Remember the poor. In Galatians 2, the Apostle Paul recounts his meeting with the Jerusalem Council (see Acts 15) regard-

ing the message he was preaching to the Gentiles. The Council affirmed Paul's message and ministry to the Gentiles and asked only
"that we should continue to remember the poor, the very thing I
(Paul) was eager to do" (Gal. 2:10). Given the serious divisions between Jews and Gentiles, this was a remarkable statement. The one
important thing was to continue remembering the poor.

James: Look after orphans and widows. The book of James is full
of practical wisdom and directives about how we should act out our
faith in treatment of others. In the first chapter James states, "Religion that God our Father accepts as pure and faultless is this: to look
after orphans and widows in their distress and to keep oneself from
being polluted by the world" (James 1:27). In the second chapter,
James talks about not showing favoritism for the wealthy over the
poor. He writes:

*My brothers, as believers in our glorious Lord Jesus Christ, don't show favorit-
ism. Suppose a man comes into your meeting wearing a gold ring and fine
clothes, and a poor man in shabby clothes also comes in. If you show special
attention to the man wearing fine clothes and say, "Here's a good seat for
you," but say to the poor man, "You stand there" or "Sit on the floor by my feet,"
have you not discriminated among yourselves and become judges with evil
thoughts? (James 2:1-4).*

BIBLICAL INTERPRETATION: THE PROBLEM OF CULTURAL BLINDNESS

Matthew Henry (1662-1714), a Presbyterian minister famous for his
commentary on the Old and New Testament, writes about the James passage quoted above:

*But we must be careful not to apply what is here said to the common assem-
blies for worship; for in these certainly there may be appointed different places
of persons according to their rank and circumstances, without sin* (Henry
1949).

On what bases did Matthew Henry come to this conclusion, in direct
contradiction the plain meaning of James? There is no scriptural support
for continuing a practice that treats people differently according to their
socioeconomic class, race or other features. Yet Matthew Henry was, in
this particular instance, blinded by the practices of the society in which he

lived. Matthew Henry wrote at a time when blacks in the United States were required to sit in a separate location from whites. According to DeYoung "African Americans were relegated to back pews, galleries, roof pews, separate balconies, standing along the rear wall, or even listening from outside the building"(DeYoung, Emerson et al. 2003, 49).

Leith Anderson, president of the National Association of Evangelicals, said, "Most evangelical churches are "Bible-driven, not current events-driven"(Goodstein and Banerjee). The trouble is not with churches being "Bible-driven," but with not giving cultural practices and current-events the recognition they deserve as strong influences in the day to day world where we live out our faith. This was the case with Matthew Henry's non-application of the James passage above. We need to examine how we are living in light of scriptural truths with the humble awareness that we can easily fool ourselves into thinking that we are living out Scriptural principles better than we really are.

Alister McGrath, Professor of Theology, Ministry and Education, and Head of the Centre for Theology, Religion and Culture at King's College, London calls attention to this problem:

> Biblical passages are treated as timeless and culture-free statements that can be assembled to yield a timeless and culture-free theology that stands over and above the shifting sands of our postmodern culture (Perry 2002, 55).

The Bible was written in a specific time period and culture and that context must be understood in order to apply the Scripture to our own circumstances. When it comes to our acting upon principles taught in the Bible, it must always be in light of both the Biblical and our particular, present-day situation. Understanding our cultural blinders means that we will also try to study and apply scripture from as many perspectives as we can. When we study with people from other classes and ethnic groups and read their writings, we gain a different and fuller understanding of the text.

God's desire for unity among his followers, and justice for the oppressed, is clear in both the Old and the New Testaments. Living as "one" means that we must make every effort to overcome, with God's help, those things that separate us for the sake of the gospel. In most instances, multiethnic congregations are God's will for us. (See Appendix 3 for an articulation of the case for exceptions). God has created all people in his image and they must be treated with worth, dignity and significance (Gen. 1:27). Moreover, the effectiveness of our Christian witness is dependent on our love and unity (John 13:34-35; 17:20-21). Finally, the "mystery" revealed in the New Testament is that all people should believe, obey and worship God (Rom. 16:25-27; Eph. 2:11-3:13). Jesus broke down the greatest ethnic divide in the Bible, between Jews and Gentiles, so that we would no longer live as two but one. God wants his children today to also overcome anything that divides us. He wants us to have the joy of rich, cross-cultural relationships in Christ and for the quality of our love for one another to proclaim loudly the transforming power of the gospel.

APPENDIX 2

ETHNIC COMPOSITION OF AMHERST CHRISTIAN FELLOWSHIP, 1993 - 2005

YEAR	Overall	Asian American	Black/ African American	Inter-national	Hispanic/ Latino American	Multi-racial	White
1993	32	8	1	1	3	0	19
1994	40	10	4	2	1	0	23
1995	44	12	10	4	1	0	17
1996	61	16	12	6	6	0	26
1997	83	20	15	12	10	0	26
1998	53	18	7	7	2	0	19
1999	56	19	10	6	3	3	15
2000	31	7	6	8	0	0	10
2001	42	8	8	5	0	1	20
2002	48	16	9	6	1	0	16
2003	65	21	11	4	3	1	25
2004	66	14	10	8	3	2	29
2005	90	27	12	6	4	5	36

Note: No student self-identified as Native American between 1993-2005, and for that reason Native American does not appear here as a category. Some students listed under multiracial identified as part American Indian or Mexican Indian.

Appendix 3

A case for continuing monoethnic minority fellowships

Reverend Timothy Jones

When the words came out of my mouth I wished that I could bring them back. There I was sitting in the middle of a debate in my seminary class entitled "Race and American Christianity" and I said it, "Any monoethnic church in a multiethnic neighborhood is sinful." I had just recently come home from a conference on multiethnic ministry and I was especially passionate at this point. My already strong feelings in support of multiethnic ministry had been intensified by a charismatic and bold keynote speaker. In retrospect, I see that my words lacked compassion and skill. As soon as I said them, I could feel the reaction from two of my sisters in the class. Two young women, good friends of mine, ladies that I look up to as big sisters in the faith, African American sisters, immediately reacted with vehemence and zeal. I could hear a sense of betrayal in their voices, as if I had just committed treason. How could I, a son of the traditional Black Church, make such a comment? What I remember the most is the emotion in their voices and the pain on their faces as they rebutted my statement, and rhetorically ripped me to shreds. In the heat of the argument I refused to change my position. But as I drove home from class that day, I pondered my statement and the reaction that it evoked. Was I wrong? Was my statement unfair? Why were my two sisters so offended? I thought and prayed about this issue long after that conversation. While I have not wavered in my commitment to multiethnic ministry, I can now honestly affirm the importance of monoethnic minority fellowships as well.

It is somewhat uncomfortable for me to challenge the clear call that has been made throughout this book for multiethnic fellowships. God's word gives this call to fellowship, worship, and serve across cultures to everyone. However, considering the racial makeup of our country, its history of racism, and its rich traditions of monoethnic minority ministry, I do believe that there is still a place for these types of fellowships to continue.

We need both monoethnic and multiethnic fellowships; these two types of situations can work in concert with one another. This is certainly the model of InterVarsity Christian Fellowship on many college campuses. InterVarsity is a campus ministry committed to multiethnic ministry but its leaders still cultivate ethnic specific fellowships—Black Campus Ministries, LaFe (Latino Fellowship), and Asian American Ministries. During my time at Amherst I was a part of the Amherst Christian Fellowship, a large multiethnic Christian group, as well as a member of the Mrs. Hermenia T. Gardener Bi-Semester Christian Worship series, a committee committed to putting on an African American styled worship experience twice during each semester. As much as I embraced the idea of multiethnic fellowships, I always felt especially renewed and energized whenever we had a service in the tradition that I grew up in. It takes real work to be in multiethnic worship environments; sometimes it is refreshing to be in worship settings where I am not constantly uncomfortable.

Churches that are founded and committed to multiethnic ministry might still encourage ethnic specific gatherings within their congregations. We are one body, joined in one baptism, with one Spirit, but there is something unique that happens in an ethnic specific environment. In the same way that many churches have age specific or "life stage specific" small groups—young parents, singles, empty nesters—churches might consider encouraging ethnic specific groups within their multiethnic congregations to provide a place of support and comfort for the minority members of their congregation.

Ethnic specific churches have historically served as a place of cultural cultivation and identity affirmation. It is in the black church that I first learned that God made me black on purpose, and that I can be proud of how God made me. Who I am as a person was forged within the confines of an ethnic specific congregation. In a country where the worth of many minorities is often put into question, monoethnic churches have served as a place where people are affirmed in their God given ethnicities. Stated differently, monoethnic churches often create a sense of "somebodyness" for ethnic minorities. Regardless of how individuals might be viewed and treated throughout the week, their monoethnic congregation can be a place where they feel like a person, feel like somebody, and are affirmed as such. Before any of us can move towards reconciliation, we must have peace regarding our own ethnic identities and racial heritage. Reconciliation cannot happen if the individuals involved do not love themselves.

Monoethnic congregations have served as a place of real comfort for many Christians. Most minorities are deeply involved with the majority culture throughout their week, often causing great stress. Many look forward to their worship experience and church participation as a time where they don't have to pay the cost of majority culture involvement. In other words, many minority Christians expect worship to be a time when they can relax and put down the guard that they have up throughout their week.

One of the points that my sisters made in that classroom confrontation was that some people were not ready to worship in multiethnic environments due to long standing hurt across races. It stands to reason that people who fall into this category may not be immediately comfortable moving into a multiethnic environment. A slow and gradual process of reconciliation may be necessary for some minority individuals before they could become healthy and participating members of a multiethnic congregation. This is not to diminish or modify the gospel call to reconciliation, but simply to allow for a "baby steps" approach to this great work. Practically speaking, forcing people who are not ready out of their monoethnic churches into multiethnic churches would cause great harm to all involved.

America's history of racism makes multiethnic fellowships difficult. As we seek to emulate the vision of the great multiethnic fellowship portrayed in Revelation 7:9—"a great multitude that no one could count, from every nation, tribe, people and language, standing before the throne and in front of the Lamb"—we must not hastily throw away the beauty and tradition of monoethnic minority fellowships. In fact, in the effort to become more multiethnic, members of the majority culture might even do well to join these types of congregations instead of expecting minorities to join their congregations. I thank God for the reaction of my sisters because it reminded me of the skill and compassion necessary to continue the work of reconciliation.

APPENDIX 4
ACTS STUDY GUIDE

ACTS 1-3

1. Analyze the plan for the spread of the Gospel in 1:8 in light of cultural considerations. To whom was this assignment given originally? What might be some anticipated obstacles in fulfilling this assignment?

2. How did culture figure into the selection of a replacement for Judas Iscariot?

3. What cultural considerations were made by the Holy Spirit on the Day of Pentecost?

4. What do you make of the listing of the nations?

5. What "culture" was created among the new believers?

6. What elements of Jewish culture were used by Peter in chapter 3?

7. Why does Peter make reference to Abraham, Isaac and Jacob in his second sermon?

ACTS 4-5

1. Culturally speaking, what surprised the religious rulers about Peter and John?

2. What "line" did Peter and John draw in their interaction with the chief priests and elders?

3. How was life together (culture!) for the early church impacted by the filling of the Spirit?

4. Where did the apostles go to teach and preach? Why?

5. Acts 6-7

6. What was the nature of the cultural conflict in Acts 6?

7. What proposal did the apostles make to solve the problem?

8. Examine the names of the men who were selected. What can you conclude about the solution to the problem?

9. What was the basis of the false charges against Stephen?

10. What did Stephen use as his defense? How was this culturally relevant?

11. What seemed to anger them most about Stephen's speech?

ACTS 8-9

1. What happened in response to persecution which broke out upon the Church?

2. Examine Philip's ministry in Samaria in cross-cultural terms.

3. Analyze the cultural implications of Philip's ministry to the Ethiopian eunuch.

4. What was to be the nature of Saul's ministry for the Lord?

5. How did Saul "begin" his ministry? What are the cultural implications?

6. What group especially wanted to kill Saul?

7. What was the nature of Tabitha's (Dorcas) ministry before she died?

ACTS 10-12

1. Examine Peter's vision in light of culture and ministry. How was God preparing Peter for what lay ahead?

2. How did Peter's ministry to Cornelius and company cross cultural boundaries?

3. What important lesson do we learn about God in Peter's own words? What are the implications for our ministries?

4. Why was there contention about Peter's ministry among the Gentiles? How did Peter defend his ministry among the Gentiles?

5. How was the Gospel spreading and how did the church in Antioch begin? What are the implications of disciples being called "Christians for the first time?"

6. Jesus called the temple "a house of prayer." Where was the prayer meeting held for Peter while he was in prison? Why is this significant?

ACTS 13-14

1. Look at the list of prophets and teachers in Ac. 13:1. How does this demonstrate the diversity of the church at Antioch?

2. What was the first stop on the first missionary journey? Why is this significant?

3. A pattern begins to emerge in the way Barnabas and Saul did ministry. What was it?

4. What approach does Paul use in his preaching at Pisidian Antioch?

5. Why was there opposition to Paul's ministry? How did Paul and Barnabas respond? How did the Gentiles respond?

6. What were the results of Paul's ministry in Iconium?

7. How was the ministry of Paul and Barnabas received in Lystra? What did they refuse to allow?

8. What missionary report did Paul give to the church at Antioch?

ACTS 15-18

1. What controversial, cultural teaching began to circulate in Antioch? Who proposed this same teaching in Jerusalem?

2. What is the essence of Peter's argument at the Jerusalem Council?

3. What is the essence of James' argument?

4. What was contained in the letter from the Council? What are the cultural implications?

5. What cultural concession did Paul make for Timothy? Why do you think he did so?

6. Where did Paul and company go in Philippi for ministry and to whom did they minister?

7. What got Paul into trouble at Philippi?

8. How did Paul and Silas handle their imprisonment? How did God use this?

9. When, where and for how long did Paul do ministry in Thessalonica? Who responded?

10. What was Paul and company accused of doing by the unbelieving Jews in Thessalonica? What did this mean?

11. What was the response to Paul's preaching in Berea? What was a contributing factor? What was this emerging church going to look like?

12. In what places did Paul proclaim the Gospel in Athens? In what ways did Paul use his cultural context to proclaim the Gospel there?

13. What social upheaval are we informed about in Acts 18? What was the difference in Paul's ministry when Silas and Timothy weren't with him and when they were with him?

14. What significant statement does Paul make to the Jews who resisted the Gospel?

15. Compare Ac. 18:2 with 18:18 and 18:26. What do you notice? What is the cultural relevance of name order?

ACTS 19-22

1. What did Paul do for three months at Ephesus? What did he do when that door closed?

2. What did many of the new converts do as a result of Paul's ministry in Ephesus? What impact did this have?

3. How did Paul describe his ministry to the Ephesians in ch. 20?

4. What cultural ritual did Paul perform at Jerusalem? Who suggested it and for what reason? How well did it work?

5. Why did the Roman commander listen to Paul?

6. In what language did Paul address the crowd? Why is this significant?

7. Why did the crowd quiet down?

8. How did Paul try to connect with the crowd? What does Paul use as his defense?

9. What caused the crowd to stop listening to Paul?

10. What kept the Romans from scourging Paul?

11. What is the significance of the difference between Paul's citizenship and that of the commander?

ACTS 23-26

1. Why does Paul show respect for the high priest?

2. How was Paul able to divide the assembly?

3. How did Paul defend himself before Felix? Why did Felix send for Paul on a number of occasions? Could Paul have obtained his freedom? What are the implications for ministry within a corrupt society?

4. What was the cultural significance of Paul's appeal to Caesar?

5. How does Paul begin his defense before King Agrippa?

6. How did Paul almost convince King Agrippa to become a Christian?

ACTS 27-28

1. How did Paul use the shipwreck for ministry?

2. Why would it have been acceptable in Roman culture to kill the prisoners rather than let them escape? What does this say about the centurion when he prevented this from being carried out?

3. What was the initial conclusion that the inhabitants of Malta came to concerning Paul? What changed this conclusion?

4. How did Paul minister to the inhabitants of Malta?

5. What was the first thing Paul did while under house arrest?

6. What did Paul do for two years while under house arrest?

APPENDIX 5
QUESTIONS FOR LISTENING

The following is an interactive exercise that we have enjoyed using in Amherst Christian Fellowship. We have often used it on retreats and it takes about an hour. We pair people up with someone they do not know well. One person simply asks questions about the other and listens, speaking only to ask a question or clarify. The other gets to tell his or her story for 30 minutes uninterrupted. Then the partners switch places. This has proven to be a wonderful way to move relationships forward.

INSTRUCTIONS

Listen to your partner for an agreed upon length of time (twenty or thirty minutes works well). Ask some of the following questions, paraphrasing them or asking questions of your own. Read the questions before you begin and mark the ones you want to be sure to use. If you have time at the end, and are comfortable, you might want to take a moment to pray for each other silently or aloud.

GROWING UP

What was your living situation like growing up?

Who were the important people and/or institutions in your life (e.g. friends, parents, teachers, school, athletic teams, scouts, church)?

When would you say that you first encountered people who were really different from yourself? What effect did that have on you?

Was there anyone of a different race than your own that significantly influenced you?

Spiritual Life & Challenges

What has been the course of your spiritual journey until now?

Have there been times in your spiritual journey that were especially important to you?

What kind of obstacles have you faced in living out your faith or other commitments (e.g. failure, doubts, questions, loss)?

Refreshment & Perseverance

What helps you to persevere and maintain your priorities and keep working toward your goals?

How do you find refreshment (emotional, physical, spiritual) when you are weary and feel depleted?

In difficult times, what has kept you going (e.g. spiritual practices, faith community, music, books, friends, family)?

Current Situation

How are things for you this week? Do you have any specific prayer requests?

WORKS CITED

Alliance, D. P. (April 2, 2008). "Crack/Cocaine Sentencing Disparity." http://www.drugpolicy.org/drugwar/mandatorymin/crackpowder. cfm (accessed November 18, 2010).

American Bar Association Presidential Advisory Council on Diversity in the Profession (October 2005). "The Critical Need to Further Diversify the Legal Academy & the Legal Profession." http://www.abanet.org/op/pipelineconf/acdreport.pdf (accessed November 18, 2010)

Bonacich, E. (October 1973). "A Theory of Middleman Minorities." *American Sociological Review* 38: 583-594.

Boorstein, M. (February 5, 2008). "Megachurch Pastor Warren Calls for a Second Reformation." Washington Post. Washington, DC.

Brown-Collins, A. (December 6, 2000). "Restructuring fellowships: Prayer in the black tradition." InterVarsity Christian Fellowship, Black Campus Ministry. Church of the Good Shepherd, Roxbury, MA.

Chin, A. (April 21, 2001) "A Brief History of the 'Model Minority' Stereotype." http://modelminority.com/joomla/index.php?option=com_content&view=article&id=113:a-brief-history-of-the-model-minority-stereotype-&catid=40:history&Itemid=56 (accessed November 10, 2010)

DeYoung, C. P., M. O. Emerson, et al. (2003). *United by faith : the multiracial congregation as an answer to the problem of race.* Oxford ; New York, Oxford University Press.

Digest, P. N. (March 13, 2008) "African-American, Latino Children more Likely Than White Children to Be Poor, Study Finds." Philanthropy News Digest: A Service of the Foundation Center.

Dovidio, J. F., S. L. Gaertner, et al. (2002). "Why Can't We Just Get Along? Interpersonal Biases and Interracial Distrust." *Cultural Diversity and Ethnic Minority Psychology* 8(2): 88-102

Ellis, C. F. J. (December 12, 2001). "Managing Diversity." InterVarsity Christian Fellowship New England Regional Staff Conference. Toah Nipi Conference Center, Rindge, NH.

Emerson, M. O. and R. M. Woo (2006). *People of the dream : multiracial congregations in the United States.* Princeton, N.J., Princeton University Press.

Emerson, M. O. and Christian Smith (2000). *Divided by Faith: Evangelical Religion and the Problem of Race in America.* New York, Oxford University Press.

FactFinder, U. S. C. B. A. (2005). "Survey: 2005 American Community Survey." http://factfinder.census.gov/ (accessed November 18, 2010).

Gilbreath, E. (2006). *Reconciliation blues : a Black evangelical's inside view of white Christianity.* Downers Grove, IL, IVP Books.

Hannah, D. (February 29, 2008) "1 in 100 Now Behind Bars; Numbers for Blacks and Latinos Bleak." Diversityinc. http://www.diversityinc.com/article/3148/1-in-100-Now-Behind-Bars-Numbers-for-Blacks-and-Latinos-Bleak/ (accessed March 8, 2008).

Helms, J. E. (1995). "An update of Helm's White and People of Color racial identity models." *Handbook of multicultural counseling.* J. G. Ponterotto, J. M. Casas, L. A. Suzuki and C. M. Alexander. Thousand Oaks, CA, Sage Publications, Inc.: 679.

Henry, M. (1949). *Matthew Henry's commentary on the whole Bible.* New York, Fleming H. Revell.

Jackson, D. Z. (2000). "If you think the MCAS history test is relevant, try this exam." *Boston Globe.* Boston: A23.

Johnson, J. R., J. W. Johnson, et al. (1970). *Lift every voice and sing.* New York, Hawthorn Books.

Jung, A. (August 29, 2007). "The Racial Divide of America's Youth: Whites Happier Than Everyone Else." AlterNet. http://www.alternet.org/bloggers/61030 (accessed March 25, 2008).

Keener, C. S. (1993). *The IVP Bible background commentary : New Testament.* Downers Grove, IL., InterVarsity Press.

Keener, C. S. (October 17, 1996). "Reaching across cultural barriers." Reconciliation: the Heart of the Gospel Conference. Amherst College.

Keener, C. S. (1997). *Matthew.* Downers Grove, IL., InterVarsity Press.

King, M. L., Jr. (1963). "Social Justice and the Emerging New Age." http://www.wmich.edu/library/archives/mlk/q-a.html (accessed September 15, 2010).

Kozol, J. (1992). *Savage inequalities : children in America's schools.* New York, HarperPerennial.

Law, E. H. F. (1993). *The Wolf Shall Dwell with the Lamb: A Spirituality of Leadership in a Multicultural Community.* St. Louis, Chalice Press.

Millman, J. (March 6, 2008). "Discrimination Charges Hit 5-Year High; Retaliation, Retaliation, Religion Set New Records." Diversityinc. http://www.diversityinc.com/article/3161/Discrimination-Charges-Hit-5Year-High-Retaliation-Religion-Set-New-Records/ (accessed March 8, 2008).

Nagasawa, M. (November 15, 2001). "Asian American Spirituality, White American Fundamentalism and White Postmodern Evangelicalism: A Dialogue." Address, Fellowship of Asian American Ministers and Ministries. HighRock Church, Somerville, MA.

Obama, B. (March 18, 2008) "Barack Obama's Speech on Race " *New York Times.*

Ohlemacher, S. (November 14, 2006). "Race still matters in poverty rates." *The Republican.* Springfield, MA: 8.

Oliver, M. L. and T. M. Shapiro (2006). *Black wealth, white wealth : a new perspective on racial inequality.* New York, NY, Routledge.

Perie, M. and R. Moran. (July 2005). "The Nation's Report Card: Long-Term Trend." http://nces.ed.gov/nationsreportcard/pubs/2005/2005464.asp (accessed October 11, 2010).

Perkins, S. and C. Rice (1993). *More than equals : racial healing for the sake of the gospel.* Downers Grove, IL., InterVarsity Press.

Perry, D. (2002). *Building unity in the church of the new millennium.* Chicago, Moody Press.

Shuker, N. (1985). *World Leaders Past and Present: Martin Luther King.* New York, Burke Publishing Company Limited.

Stott, J. R. W. (1990). *The Spirit, the church, and the world.* Downers Grove, IL., InterVarsity Press.

Sue, D. W., C. M. Capodilupo, et al. (May-June 2007). "Racial Microaggressions in Everyday Life: Implications for Clinical Practice." *American Psychologist* 62(4): 271-286.

Tatum, B. D. (1997). *"Why are all the black kids sitting together in the cafeteria?" and other conversations about race.* New York, BasicBooks.

University of Wisconsin School of Medicine and Public Health Center for the Study of Cultural Diversity in Healthcare (2008). "Health Disparity Statistics." https://ictr.wisc.edu/ (accessed March 25, 2008).

Washington, R. and G. Kehrein (1993). *Breaking Down Walls: A Model for Reconciliation in an Age of Racial Strife.* Chicago, Moody Press.

Webber, R. (June 2000). "What Does the Shift into a Postmodern Culture Mean for Worship?" Lecture, Regent College. Vancouver, BC

Williamson, P. R. (2003). *Covenant. Dictionary of the Old Testament: Pentateuch.* T. D. Alexander and D. W. Baker. Downers Grove, IL, InterVarsity Press.

Young, Y. (November 2, 2007) "Blacks, whites share favorite TV shows." *USA Today.*

CONTRIBUTING AUTHORS

SARAH BASS (B.A. Amherst College) is completing a Masters of Fine Arts in Creative Writing at the University of the West Indies in Trinidad and Tobago. In addition to serving on the leadership team at Amherst, she was an active member of Athletes in Action, a ministry directed at student athletes on campus. After graduating, Sarah taught for two years in South Los Angeles, where her commitment to justice on behalf of the poor through education reform was established.

JENNIFER ROBERGE CHUDY (B.A. Amherst College) was involved with the Amherst Christian Fellowship in a variety of leadership roles during her time at Amherst. She currently lives in Washington D.C. with her husband where she teaches computer science at a Catholic High School.

ROBERT M. GODZENO (B.A. Amherst College, J.D. Quinnipiac University School of Law) was a leader in the Amherst Christian Fellowship and played in the Amherst College Jazz Ensemble. He served as Executive Managing Editor of the Quinnipiac Law Review. Rob is now an Associate at the firm of Sullivan & Cromwell. He and his wife live in Manhattan. They are active in the First Congregational Church of Stamford, CT and also attend Marble Collegiate Church in New York.

SUE HAHN GUTIERREZ (B.A. Amherst College, M.P.P. Harvard Kennedy School of Government) is an International Economist with the U.S. Department of Labor. She works to strengthen worker rights around the world as a negotiator of international trade and investment agreements. Sue attended Amherst College and belonged to the Amherst Christian Fellowship from 1990-1994. She and her Nicaraguan husband, Alexis, and their multiracial infant daughter recently began attending a small church plant in a predominantly African American community in Washington, DC.

JANET K. HA (B.A. Amherst College) was a student leader in the Amherst Christian fellowship. After graduating, she worked as a client relationship manager for Google for three years. She is currently working on her Master of Fine Arts in fiction writing at Indiana University at Bloomington. She married Matthew Mascioli in the summer of 2009.

REVEREND TIMOTHY L. JONES (B.A. Amherst College, M.Div. Boston University School of Theology) currently serves as the Pastor of First Central Baptist Church in Chicopee, MA. He also serves part-time at Amherst College as a Protestant Advisor and Advisor to the Mrs. Hermenia T. Gardner Bi-Semester Christian Worship Series. While at Amherst College, he served on the leadership team with the Amherst Christian Fellowship. He is married to Nelly (Reyes) Jones and they have one daughter, Sofia Esperanza.

REVEREND YOLANDA DENSON LEHMAN (B.A., Wesleyan University, M.Div., Harvard University) completed her supervised internship at Amherst College and was a volunteer staff worker with the Amherst Christian Fellowship. She currently serves as the Associate Pastor at Atonement Lutheran Church in St. Cloud, Minnesota. She serves as a pastor, evangelist, and professor, and she publishes an online, daily, and Christian devotional entitled, "Ainta That Good News?!" She is married to Dr. Christopher P. Lehman and has four children.

BONNIE E. LIN (B.A. Amherst College) is a graduate student at Princeton Theological Seminary. She served on the leadership and outreach teams of the Amherst Christian Fellowship, and represented the Fellowship on the school's Multifaith Council. She was also a Peer Advocate for Sexual Respect, co-founder of North Korea Awareness Week, and tutor in the Writing Center and three local schools.

MELODY KO LIN (B.A. Amherst College) works for The Hartford as an actuary. From 2000-2004, she was part of the worship team for Amherst

Christian Fellowship. She and her husband Dan live in Connecticut where they lead worship at a predominantly Asian church.

JANET A. LYDECKER (B.A., Amherst College, M.S., Virginia Commonwealth University) was a leader in the Amherst Christian fellowship in 2005 and 2006. She is currently a doctoral student in Psychology at Virginia Commonwealth University. She is active in the Area 10 Faith Community in downtown Richmond, VA, a church focused on serving its neighbors and influencing the entire city.

JAKE MAGUIRE (B.A. Amherst College; M.A. University of Texas- Austin) was a member of the Amherst Christian Fellowship worship team from 2003-2007. He is a doctoral student in American Studies at the University of Texas. Jake has served in a variety of roles in local, state and federal politics and currently serves as Chief Communications Advisor to the 100,000 Homes Campaign. He is also a former Archer Center Graduate Fellow and currently holds the William C. Powers graduate fellowship at Texas.

MATTHEW R. MASCIOLI (B.A. Amherst College, M.Div. Gordon-Conwell Theological Seminary) held several leadership roles while a student at Amherst College and then became an InterVarsity Christian Fellowship campus staff member at Williams and Amherst Colleges. He is currently a consultant with InterVarsity in New England. He is married to Janet Ha.

JULIAN MICHAEL (B.A Amherst College) was a member of the Amherst Christian Fellowship worship team as both a student and volunteer staff from 2001-2005. He also served as a worship leader at churches in western Massachusetts and northern Virginia. He is currently a guidance counselor in Los Angeles.

JONATHAN H. PEREZ (B.A. Amherst College) was a member of the Amherst Christian Fellowship from 2004-2007 and helped to establish Amherst Homeless Connect. He worked for two years with AmeriCorps VISTA for Nehemiah Ministries, Inc. in Springfield Massachusetts. Currently he is pursuing a doctorate in Animal Behavior at the University of California at Davis.

REVEREND TYRONE A. PERKINS (B.A., Princeton University, M.Div., Seminary of the East) is the pastor of Westside Bible Baptist Church in Trenton, NJ. He worked at Bethel Seminary of the East from 1997 until 2010 as an administrator and adjunct professor of practical theology. He also served on the Bethel Anti-Racism and Reconciliation Commission of Bethel University. He has done anti-racism and diversity training for employees and churches. Tyrone is married to Janet and has six children.

LISA PISTORIO (B.A. Amherst College) played alto saxophone as part of Amherst Christian Fellowship's worship team. After graduation she worked with AmeriCorps in Washington, DC, and worked for a children's advocacy organization. She is pursuing a master's degree at Fuller Theological Seminary, where she is focusing on cross-cultural ministry with children at risk.

CHRIS RICE has served as co-director of the Duke Center for Reconciliation since 2005. He grew up in South Korea, the child of Presbyterian missionaries, and then lived and worked for 17 years in an inner-city neighborhood of Jackson, Mississippi with Voice of Calvary, an interracial church and community development ministry. Chris came to Duke Divinity School in 2000 to pursue ways for the academy to serve the world of Christian activism. He is the author of *Reconciling All Things: A Christian Vision of Justice, Peace, and Healing*; *Grace Matters*; and co-author, with Spencer Perkins, of *More Than Equals: Racial Healing for the Sake of the Gospel*. Chris is an ordained elder in the Presbyterian Church (U.S.A.). He and his wife Donna have three children.

REVEREND PAUL V. SORRENTINO (B.A. University of Rhode Island, M.A. University of Chicago, M.Div. Bethel Seminary of the East, D. Min. Princeton Theological Seminary) is Director of Religious Life at Amherst

College and a regional coordinator with InterVarsity Christian Fellowship. He was the principal staff worker for the Amherst Christian Fellowship from 1991-2005. Paul is ordained with the Conservative Congregational Christian Conference and on the faculty of Bethel Seminary of the East. He and his wife, Karen, have two sons.

ALEXIS SPENCER-BYERS (B.A. Amherst College) is a freelance writer and editor currently based in San Francisco. Immediately after graduating from Amherst, she spent fifteen years in Jackson, Mississippi, working for various community development and racial reconciliation-focused nonprofit organizations. While in Jackson, she also partnered with a friend to open Koinonia Coffee House, an establishment dedicated to nurturing multicultural community.

CHRIS TSANG (B.A. Amherst College, M.Ed. Lesley University, M.Ed. Harvard University) is an eighth grade English Language Arts teacher at the Harbor Pilot Middle School in Dorchester, MA, an inner city community in Boston. He has taught for eight years as a middle school Humanities and English teacher and plans to pursue school leadership in the future. He attends the Gathering Christian Fellowship, a multiethnic house church in Dorchester.

PAUL WHITING (B.A. Amherst College, M.D. Harvard Medical School) is a resident in Orthopaedic Surgery at Tufts Medical Center in Boston, MA, where he serves as a faculty advisor for the Christian Medical and Dental Association chapter at Tufts University. He and his wife, Gloria, live in downtown Boston.

LaVergne, TN USA
14 December 2010
208726LV00001B/2/P